BON

The L. Ron Hubbard Series

BRIDGE PUBLICATIONS, INC.
5600 E. Olympic Blvd.
Commerce, California 90022 USA

ISBN 978-1-4031-9879-2

© 1996, 2012 L. Ron Hubbard Library. All Rights Reserved.

Any unauthorized copying, translation, duplication, importation or distribution, in whole or in part, by any means, including electronic copying, storage or transmission, is a violation of applicable laws.

Special acknowledgment is made to the L. Ron Hubbard Library for permission to reproduce photographs from his personal collection. Additional credits: pp. 1, 17, 53, 69, 91, 99, 117, back cover Makhnach/Shutterstock.com; pp. 25, 26, 43, 48, 49, 84, 85, 93–95, 102, 103, 110–113 Bruno Ferrari/Shutterstock.com; pp. 29, 31–45, 47–49, 57–64, 73–82 EcOasis/Shutterstock.com; p. 56 Peter Stackpole/Time & Life Pictures/Getty Images; p. 90 upper left RDA/Getty Images; p. 90 upper right Derek Colmer/Hulton Archive/Getty Images; p. 90 center left General Photographic Agency/Getty Images; p. 90 center right Keystone/Getty Images; p. 90 lower Brooke/Getty Images; pp. 96 & 97 Kenneth V. Pilon/Shutterstock.com; p. 104 Michael S. Quinton/National Geographic/Getty Images; pp. 108 & 109 George F. Mobley/National Geographic/Getty Images.

Articles and Illustrations: pp. 49, 88 & 89, 91, 93–95 *Argosy Magazine* are © 1936, 1937 Argosy Communications, Inc. All Rights Reserved. Reprinted with permission from Argosy Communications, Inc.

Dianetics, Scientology, L. Ron Hubbard, LRH, Hubbard and *Ron Signature* are trademarks and service marks owned by Religious Technology Center and are used with its permission.

Scientologist is a collective membership mark designating members of the affiliated churches and missions of Scientology.

Bridge Publications, Inc. is a registered trademark and service mark in California and it is owned by Bridge Publications, Inc.

NEW ERA is a trademark and service mark owned by New Era Publications International ApS and is registered in Denmark, among other countries.

Printed in the United States of America

The L. Ron Hubbard Series: Adventurer/Explorer—English

The L. Ron Hubbard Series

ADVENTURER EXPLORER
DARING DEEDS & UNKNOWN REALMS

PUBLICATIONS, INC.®

CONTENTS

Adventurer/Explorer: Daring Deeds & Unknown Realms

An Introduction to L. Ron Hubbard | 1

The Caribbean Expedition | 17
    A Salty Memo | 25
    A Sample Pick Saga *by L. Ron Hubbard* | 29
    Buried Alive! | 49

An Introductory Word on "Spinning In" | 53
    Spinning In *by L. Ron Hubbard* | 57

An Introductory Word on "Tailwind Willies" | 69
    Tailwind Willies *by L. Ron Hubbard* | 73
    "Flash" Hubbard | 84

The "Hell Job" Series | 91

The Explorers Club | 99
    A Prefatory Word from the Editor of
    Through Hell and High Water | 103
    It Bears Telling *by L. Ron Hubbard* | 105
    Recipes for Adventure | 110

Mission into Time | 117

Epilogue | 131

Appendix
    Glossary | 135
    Index | 175

An Introduction to
L. Ron Hubbard

"Have you ever been on a frontier? Have you ever felt valued for yourself just because you are a lonely man in a lonely land and met with one such as you? Have you ever felt the clannishness of frontiersmen, the warm faith in the might of the friend beside you? For the world out there, when it was lonely, when it was new, demanded certain things of the individual or else he lived not long and amongst the things demanded were a certain courage and a certain camaraderie. Men had to be big or fall before the unknown." —L. Ron Hubbard

Included here are tales from some forty years of adventure and exploration in lonely places where men lived not long without courage and camaraderie. As a preliminary word, let us bear in mind that if L. Ron Hubbard has since become synonymous with grand exploration, it is only a consequence of having explored so many far-flung lands through a greater quest for answers now found in Scientology. Let us further bear in mind the goal had never been adventure *per se,* but merely "I have gone through the world studying Man in order to understand him and *he,* not my adventures in doing so, is the important thing." Nor had he ever intended to make a legend of himself and, in fact, had only rarely discussed these matters. Finally, let us understand that the whole of Ron's existence

Left Guam, 1927: "Have you ever been on a frontier?"—LRH

Left
Dreams of Flight: photograph by L. Ron Hubbard

An Introduction to L. Ron Hubbard   1

Above
Astride Nancy Hanks, Montana, 1914

Right
A young Ron Hubbard and father in the Nevada badlands, 1920—of which an older Ron Hubbard would write: "Going across the great deserts in a car of those days on the roads of those days *was* an adventure"

was an adventure and what appears here are but selections and accounts of key endeavors. Yet with all that established and remembering, as he so neatly phrased it, "What is life without challenge?" let us now proceed.

As a broad introductory word, we might best be served by a few biographical notes Ron himself passed on to readers of *Adventure* magazine in the fall of 1935. To begin with, he explains, "I was born in Nebraska and three weeks later went to Oklahoma," where, we might add, his grandfather had established a horse ranch and where he took his first steps before the age of one. From Oklahoma, he next moved on to the state of Montana where, as he quipped, "they say I showed some signs of settling down, but I think this is merely rumor." Then came several notable adventures, including an extraordinary friendship with a Blackfoot medicine man and eventual acceptance as a tribal blood brother. He was also breaking range broncs at an early age and narrowly escaping a pack of coyotes astride a mare named Nancy Hanks—a particularly telling event for the fact it was not initially believed. Hence his later admission, "I had my adventures, but I learned to tell the lesser tale."

Above
Ron (front and center at left) leads a party of mountaineers to the lip of a glacier in the great Cascades, Washington State, 1923

Right
On the trail to becoming America's youngest Eagle Scout, 1923

The next event of note, he rightly described as an automotive *adventure* and recounted a hair-raising journey through the Rocky Mountains in his grandfather's Model T Ford. The roads, at best, were paved with sand, and generally little more than winding deer trails above a sheer abyss. Then followed equally challenging treks across Nevada deserts (where water went to the radiator and the tires blew out every thirty miles) before finally arriving in San Diego, where his father served in the United States Navy aboard a destroyer and photographs show Ron fully at home on the decks.

Although the story of L. Ron Hubbard as America's youngest Eagle Scout is fairly well known, the broad strokes should be recounted here if only as a prelude to what follows. Having entered Scouting in 1923, he soon led Washington, DC's Troop 10 to victory in regional Scouting competitions and otherwise distinguished himself entirely. That he additionally represented American Scouting at the White House and shook the hand of President Calvin Coolidge is of lesser import. But in either case, the thirteen-year-old L. Ron Hubbard had become a reasonably famous figure in fairly adventurous circles. Moreover, and more to the point, he possessed a dozen practical skills—from first aid to field cookery—to see him through forthcoming adventures.

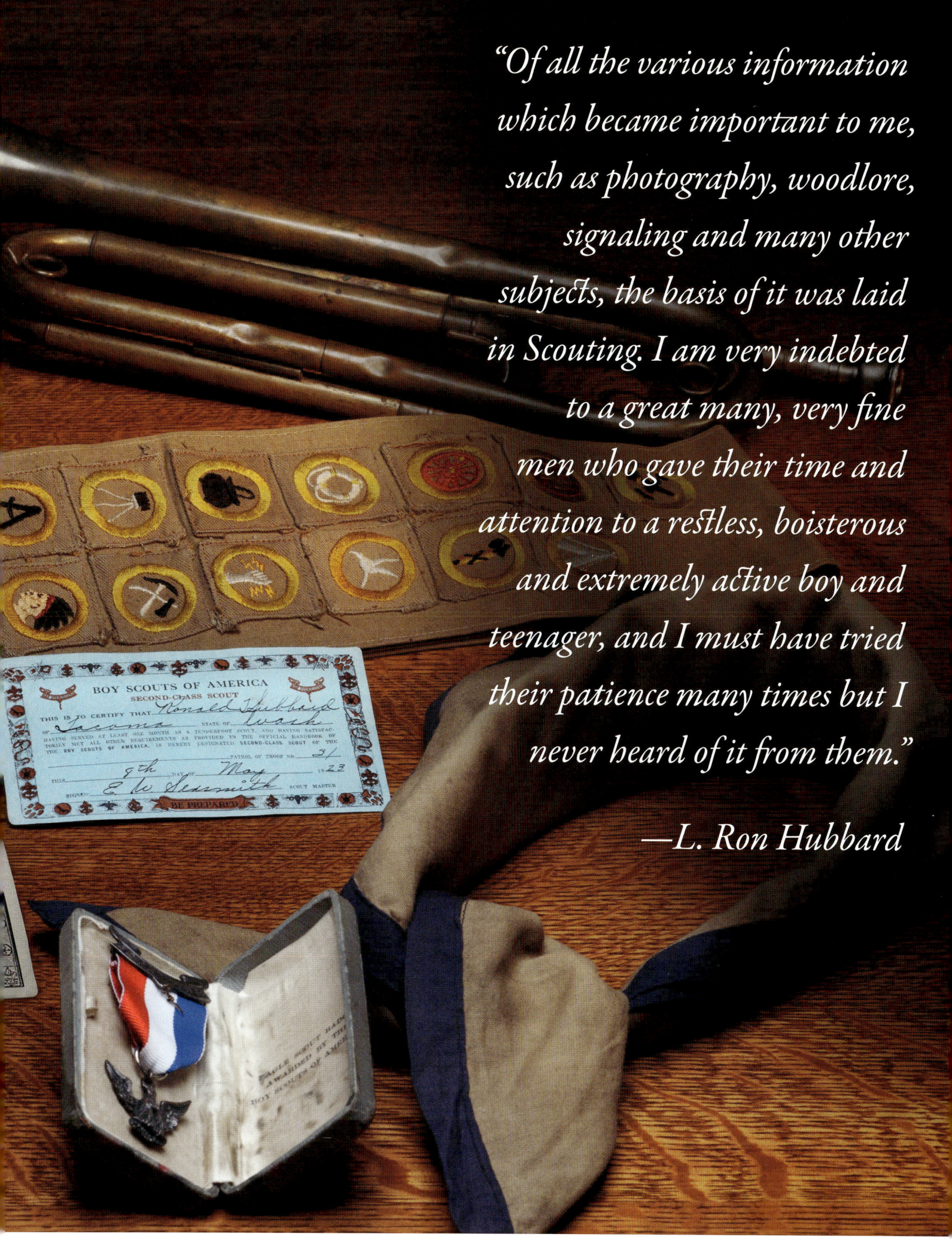

"Of all the various information which became important to me, such as photography, woodlore, signaling and many other subjects, the basis of it was laid in Scouting. I am very indebted to a great many, very fine men who gave their time and attention to a restless, boisterous and extremely active boy and teenager, and I must have tried their patience many times but I never heard of it from them."

—L. Ron Hubbard

Above
L. Ron Hubbard's major travels, 1911–1929

What amounted to the next of those adventures came in 1927 with the first of two Pacific voyages to Asia. Again, much has been said of Ron's Asian journeys: how he made his way to the island of Guam, where his father served at the United States refueling station; how from Guam he braved typhoons aboard a working schooner to finally land on the China coast; how he then made his way inland to finally venture deep into forbidden Buddhist lamaseries; and how the whole of it figured into the larger quest from whence came Dianetics and Scientology. What is not generally known, however, and is particularly relevant here, are the incidental details.

For example, among those encountered through the course of his second Asian adventure (commencing in 1928 and following a stint with Montana's 163rd National Guard) was a Major Ian Macbean of the British Secret Service. Precisely why this Macbean would take a seventeen-year-old L. Ron Hubbard

8   THE L. RON HUBBARD SERIES | *Adventurer/Explorer*

through a tour of British Intelligence efforts between Peking and Manchuria is not known. Nonetheless, and as we shall see, Macbean's lessons were to serve Ron well. Also through these Asian travels came Ron's encounter with Cantonese pirates, the engineering of a jungle road across Guam's denser corner and the evening he decked an Italian swordsman named Giovinni. (Although not before he took a saber cut across the left cheek and Macbean nearly lost a hand.)

LRH confidant and British agent extraordinaire, Ian Macbean

An Introduction to L. Ron Hubbard   9

Above
Great Wall of China near Nan-k'ou Pass, 1928; photograph by L. Ron Hubbard

Right
The Orientalist in a Peking winter, 1928

Upon his return to the United States in late 1929, and through brief service with the award-winning 20th Marines, Ron resumed his formal education to eventually enter George Washington University. (He studied engineering between other more adventurous pursuits of which we shall examine in pages to follow.) But continuing with the broad strokes, as he informed readers of *Adventure:* "Civil engineering seemed very handsome at the time. I met the lads in their Stetsons from Crabtown to Timbuktu and they seemed to lead a very colorful existence squinting into their transits. However, too late, I was sent up to Maine by the Geological Survey to find the lost Canadian border. Much bitten by seven kinds of insects, gummed by the muck of swamps, fed on johnny cake and tarheel, I saw instantly that a civil engineer had to stay far too long in far too few places and so I rapidly forgot my calculus and slipstick and began to plot ways and means to avoid the continuance of my education."

In fact, the discontinuance of his university education involved far more than mere wanderlust and had everything to do with mainline research toward the development of Dianetics and Scientology. Then, too, with Ron's departure from George Washington University came his first formal exploratory expeditions and all those expeditions yielded in purely material terms, including: LRH maritime notations still found in America's National Archives from his 1932 Caribbean expedition, the British Columbian coast pilots still bearing LRH notations from his 1940 Alaskan expedition, and all else still recorded in the annals of the famed New York Explorers Club. Yet lest we get ahead of our story, let us close this introduction with a simple reminder: we are indeed about to enter lands where "Men had to be big or fall before the unknown." ■

A rare view of China's Great Wall variously reprinted in geography texts of the day; photograph by L. Ron Hubbard

Doris Hamlin, full sail on Chesapeake Bay at the start of the Caribbean Motion Picture Expedition

CHAPTER ONE

The
CARIBBEAN
EXPEDITION

The Caribbean Expedition

NOT LONG AFTER THE COMMENCEMENT OF THE SPRING semester, 1932, various American university campuses saw the posting of the following: "Restless young men with wanderlust wanted for the Caribbean Motion Picture Expedition. Cost to applicant $250 payable at the dock in Baltimore before sailing. Must be healthy, dependable, resourceful, imaginative, and adventurous. No tea-hounds or tourist material need apply."

Would-be wayfarers were directed to contact a Mr. Philip W. Browning of Port Huron, Michigan, or Mr. L. Ron Hubbard of Washington, DC. Respondents were further informed this Caribbean expedition would set sail aboard a motorless four-masted schooner—actually one of the last of such schooners—and involve the filming of pirate haunts for movie house newsreels. Among other projected ports of call were the islands of Bermuda, Martinique, St. Thomas, St. Croix, Jamaica and Puerto Rico. Also of interest was what Ron described as "data concerning the terrain and inhabitants of these little-civilized islands," as well as photographs from the rim of active volcanos—for but a modest investment of $250 per student. Not advertised, but immediately plain to all participants, were the financial difficulties in launching such a voyage through the depths of the Great Depression. Then, too, it was to be a wholly independent venture—manned, funded and directed by the fifty-six students themselves. Nevertheless, and

Left Caribbean Expedition Director, Captain L. Ron Hubbard

Below Doris Hamlin, as she appeared to the first members of the Caribbean Motion Picture Expedition

notwithstanding all attendant difficulties, including dishonest chandlers and recalcitrant leasing agents, this was the Caribbean Motion Picture Expedition.

Admittedly, it was a bold plan. Ron himself described it as audacious and spoke of a dozen troublesome details—from the leasing of 35mm cameras for that newsreel footage to the purchasing of stores. (Among other mishaps, he would tell of an enthusiastic but hapless undergraduate purchasing a thousand cases of tomato catsup instead of the thousand called-for tomatoes. Meanwhile another overly enthusiastic adventurer blew out the water tanks after plugging the vents and letting loose with a high-pressure filling hose.) Then there was the vessel itself—the 205-foot *Doris Hamlin,* still stinking from her previous cargo of livestock and vaguely known in nautical circles for having been blown farther off course than any ship in recorded history. Finally, there was the last-minute illness of fellow adventurer and expedition co-director Philip Browning, leaving Ron without his cinematographic

Above
Raising sails in the Atlantic

Left
The sun-swept deck of the *Doris Hamlin* in the Caribbean; photograph by L. Ron Hubbard

Above
Route of the Caribbean Motion Picture Expedition

equipment and otherwise shouldering the burden alone.

The first leagues were equally trying with sail-shredding winds off Chesapeake Bay and serious leaks in the aforementioned water tanks. Then followed difficulties with the native cook, necessitating an LRH hand in the galley, while the *Doris Hamlin*'s dour Captain Garfield proved himself far less than the advertised Captain Courageous, further necessitating an LRH hand at both the helm and charts, where his notations would ultimately augment coast pilots of the Lesser Antilles. Finally, in a telltale letter from Bermuda, where eleven of the party called it quits, came LRH references to tainted beef, contrary tides and financial resources as "frail and frayed" as the *Hamlin*'s sails.

Above left
Repairing blown-out sails

Above right
Raising topsails

Left
Land's end after the one grand adventure in the twilight of their youth

"It never rains but it pours," Ron quipped from Puerto Rico and told of unexpected towage costs and harbor fees. Then, too, Garfield had shredded both the foresail and flying jib, which effectively ended the *Hamlin*'s voyage and left her with a "bundle of rags" for sails. Yet in what amounted to a closing note, Ron also told of fishing for barracuda in the Sargasso Sea, plowing an exquisite Vieques Sound for coral specimens and, most significantly, ascending to the fiery mouth of Mount Pelée for a very rare photographic vista.

By way of a historical note, Pelée had indeed proven a most savage volcano—last erupting in 1902, utterly destroying the town of Saint-Pierre and killing some thirty thousand inhabitants. Otherwise, the following LRH remarks drawn from the transcript of a 1935

The Caribbean Expedition   21

Above
Two approaches to Martinique's volcano, Mount Pelée

Far left
Caribbean Expedition members ascend the slopes of a smoldering Mount Pelée, 1932

radio broadcast can hardly be improved upon:

"I was down in Martinique, that sullen black island, and I wanted a glimpse of the savage volcano Pelée which, today, is a smoldering, angry peak overshadowing the calm blue Caribbean. Occasionally it spews forth molten, boiling rock and tries again to repeat itself. It is half alive, but there is never any knowing when it will explode again.

"I was very interested in Pelée and I went to Saint-Pierre one afternoon to climb it. No one told me that it was farther than it looked and that darkness would catch hold of me. And that lava rolled down the slopes. From sheer ignorance, I started up.

"It was almost dark when I reached the top. My shoes were burned black, I had laid my socks on a rock to dry and the rock had burned them completely up. I was drenched by sudden rains and half-suffocated with fumes. It was dark when I started down. Pelée decided to have some fun with me.

"Great boulders weighing many tons began to roll, glowing and thundering down the slopes. It was necessary to dodge and dodge fast to keep from being mangled. I lost count of the narrow squeaks. The sky glowed a sullen red from the crater. Sparks flew from the bouncing boulders. Rocks pulsated with heat all about me. But I got down all right and I looked and felt like I'd been through the nether regions."

As for what else might be said about this Caribbean Motion Picture Expedition, those photographs from Mount Pelée were eventually purchased by the *New York Times*, those Vieques Sound coral specimens were finally acquired by the National Museum, and even some fifty years later, those who sailed with L. Ron Hubbard in 1932 would still speak of that voyage as the one grand adventure in the twilight of their youth. ▪

Last of the four-masted schooners and a grand if temperamental lady

A Salty Memo

On the eve of departure from the Baltimore docks, all those manning Ron's Caribbean Motion Picture Expedition received his appropriate "salty memo."

CARIBBEAN MOTION PICTURE
EXPEDITION
2124 I ST. NW. TEL. WEST 0938
WASHINGTON, D.C.
JUNE FOURTH—1932

GENTLEMEN:

It is desired that all men be aboard and stowed away before the evening of June eighteenth. And it is advised that every man jack report the seventeenth as he will have to get his uniforms, dunnage, and chaw stowed as well as procured. Furthermore, there're supplies to be loaded, boards to be nailed, wires to be strung, pulled and coiled, and the three thousand some odd (no doubt) details to be attended to, which always hoist their distress pennants the last moment.

Please advise immediately as to the size, amount and type of film you will use on the expedition. It will be packed specially with the main shipment.

Pennsylvania Railroad has lent a hand to the worried progenitors of this cruise and is writing every man his iron horse directions. All baggage should be shipped via Pa. RR to Baltimore care of the C.M.P. Expedition.

Nobody cares besides yourselves what, which, or how much baggage you bring with you. Most of it will probably be left in Baltimore, anyway. Please expect to get these "uniforms" from the slop chests of Pratt Street. The layout is the most practical and most serviceable you can get. And the cost the least. Tuxedos, overcoats and mittens should be omitted from the personal list. Only earmuffs are needed as self-protection against the biting, seafaring language.

DORIS will have no library, so a few books, especially a few dealing with the bold, bad buccaneers, will be a good addition to m'lord's wardrobe.

Include Bermuda in the itinerary. At least you had better, for Captain Garfield has.

Incidental expenses on the cruise will probably amount to beer (if you drink beer), cigarettes (if you are too proud to pirate pipe tobacco from the natives), parrots ($00.01 a ton), bananas ($00.0001 a shipload), and knickknacks (if you're the kind of a sailor with a girl in every…) Your film, its development and printing will be yours at cost.

There's only one big thing to remember, me buckos, and if you don't believe me you'll rot in irons forever and ever and ever. When we're away from these glorious United States on the twentieth of June, you'll only have one royalty, one deity, and one master—Captain Garfield.

Above "No tea-hounds or tourist material need apply"—LRH

But believe me, Gentlemen Rovers, when I say that he is fair. He'll take us out and bring us back but woe betide him who violates the laws of the sea and says "Sure, pal," instead of "Aye aye! Sir!" The directors and the staff and the complement are brothers under the skin.

Communications will be arranged through the Hartford Radio Relay League, and our position will be published daily in the shipping news. So you can get your letters and so on without a hitch. Advise your friends to get in touch with the League (Hartford, Conn) and the steamship companies who will haul the mailbags.

Yoho and a bottle of rum, see you rolling up the dock—you landlubber!

LRH of CMPE

Right Hard weather on the Atlantic while en route to Martinique; photograph by L. Ron Hubbard

Notes on "A Sample Pick Saga"

Among other lesser tales from Ron's first Caribbean voyage was an evening spent in the port of San Juan, Puerto Rico, listening to accounts of alluvial gold in the Puerto Rican hinterland. Add to such stories, the fact his Caribbean Motion Picture Expedition had finally cost him dearly, what with the assumption of Phil Browning's debts, that his father had long dreamed of augmenting his lieutenant's pay with a mining venture and a bit of investment capital from like-minded officers—and suddenly we have the makings of Ron's second voyage into the southern latitudes.

His formal account of this Puerto Rican Mineralogical Expedition (also known as the West Indies Mineralogical Expedition) he aptly entitled "A Sample Pick Saga" for the prospector's requisite tool. To all that he offers in broad strokes, let us add a few more incidental notes. Although his tone remains breezy throughout, in fact Puerto Rico proved grueling and Ron would long keep bottles of quinine at hand for recurrent bouts of malaria. Notwithstanding his failure to find that legendary lode of "metallic sunshine," the venture did indeed prove profitable with the staking of claims to silicon, manganese and several lesser ores. His references to the jibaros are significant, for he conducted much ethnological work amongst interior villages, with particular regard to that curious blend of Catholicism and voodoo known as espiritismo. Finally, let us reiterate that this Puerto Rican expedition constituted the first complete mineralogical survey under United States jurisdiction and is otherwise still remembered in the annals of grand adventure.

A SAMPLE PICK SAGA

by L. Ron Hubbard

BEACHCOMBING SOURDOUGHS HAVE SOUGHT the illusive gold throughout the West Indies since the day the Conquistadores deserted the islands for the more fruitful fields and festering swamps of Central and South America. Each valley in the Antilles seems to harbor a legend concerning the Americanos who spent their fortunes and sometimes their lives in their feverish hunt.

The archives of the country islands are crammed with receipts for the gold bullion which gorged the coffers of medieval Spain and kept alive her glory, and we go upon the theory that it was not possible for the Spaniards to have exhausted the entire mineral wealth of the islands—and the tap of the sample pick is accordingly heard from Cuba to Trinidad—although West Indian bonanzas still belong to a hazy future.

However, to go gold prospecting in the wake of the Conquistadores, on the hunting grounds of the pirates in the islands which still reek of Columbus is romantic, and I do not begrudge the sweat which splashed in the muddy rivers, and the bits of khaki which have probably blown away from the thorn bushes long ago.

This West Indian gold crusade had been going on for several centuries before it came to my notice and it would probably have gone right on without me, quite undisturbed, had it not been for a series of events which turned my fortunes inside out and faced me with the proposition of making a million.

Left Collecting samples near Corozal, 1932; photograph by L. Ron Hubbard

Above
Ron's West Indies Mineralogical Expedition route to Puerto Rico

Above
Members of a wildcat mining company along the Corozal River, 1932; photograph by L. Ron Hubbard

When the million-dollar problem arose, I ransacked my memory and recalled a small unpainted table in a ramshackle dive in San Juan, Puerto Rico where a soldier of fortune of Latin America, slightly voluble with White Horse, had whiled the time by spinning me yarn after yarn about prospectors, natives with gold pans, tons of Spanish bullion, slaves with leather sacks hauling dirt to the riversides to the crack of a Spanish whip, and Americanos picking fabulous float from rivers which glittered with gold and silver awaiting the inroads of feverish gold hunters from the north.

This incident had occurred while I was directing a motion picture expedition in the West Indies. My mining engineer called himself J. B. Carper of Washington, D.C., and boasted acquaintance with most of the Hammonds and Joplins of the mining world. He was impressive enough at sight, for his eyes were a baby-blue, and his excessive paunch invited trust. We equipped ourselves with mining pans, a sample pick, a few chemicals and acids, and decided that we were prepared for the worst. Eight hundred dollars had been raised for grubstake, and due to his elderly, responsible look, the money was duly entrusted to the engineer. That was a serious mistake, but then to place even such a small sum in the hands of a youth just turned twenty-one is not a common practice and I was forced to content myself with the arrangements.

Upon our arrival in Puerto Rico, the head of the Bureau of Commerce of the island's government was encouraging. He quoted several documents which had to do with Spanish bullion, showed us papers handed to him by his minerals committee and gave us, as a guide, the "live-wire" of the committee—a little Englishman who told stories of extreme interest if not of extreme truth.

A Sample Pick Saga   31

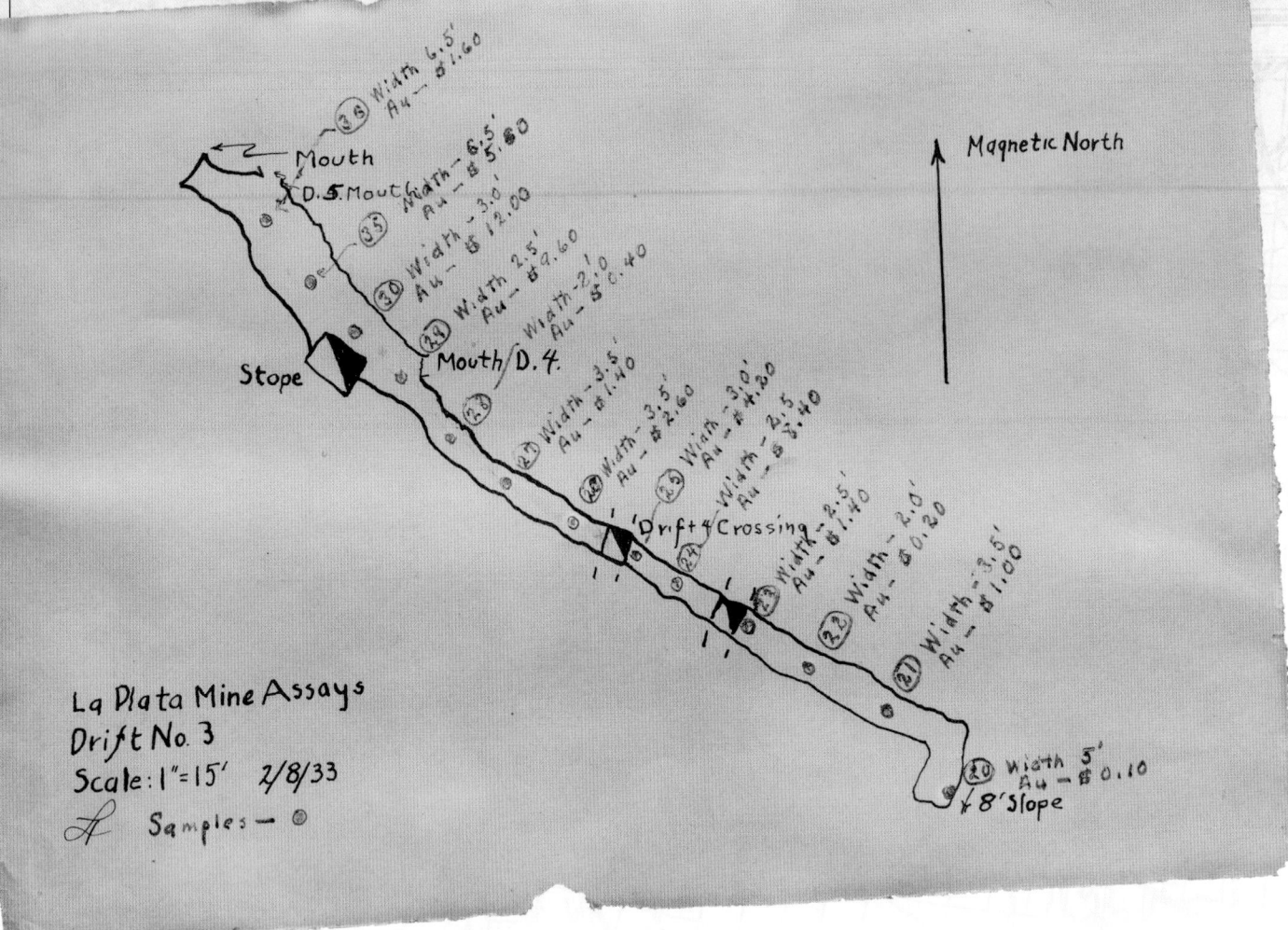

The fact that he became confidential with my engineer to the exclusion of my ears did not, at first, strike me as unusual.

But it was not the Englishman who gave me the really colorful pictures of the island's mineral past. That was left to the Spanish volubility of the esteemed Don Martin Ibanez who acted in the self-appointed capacity of the Corozal Chamber of Commerce, and a native practical miner named Jose Rodriguez.

Corozal, which became our headquarters, lies deep in the mountains southwest of San Juan. It is the center of a district of five rivers, all of which bear alluvial gold. Many natives of the village make their living by indolent panning in these streams. Several mining men had come and gone leaving either debts or their meager funds in the basin.

Perhaps the most colorful of these prospectors was a once-wealthy northerner named Sayer who had died in the town some years before our debut, though the monuments to his follies still stand and his little Dutch house—built in defiance of tropical heat—still faces the public square. He had spent fifty thousand dollars, twenty years, and finally his life, in his search for metallic sunshine, but we were heartily assured that only his own foolishness had prevented him from uncovering a vast fortune.

Don Martin spoke excellent Castile, and I was not too tried in understanding him, but Don Jose had lost his teeth back in the early days of his prospecting career, and the hillman language lisped would have been impossible had it not been for the arm waving and excruciating pantomime which accompanied each of his stories. In Jose's stories of Sayer, he would imitate the Americano's method of speech, and as Sayer had forgotten most of the English language during his long stay in Corozal, the result was ear-splitting.

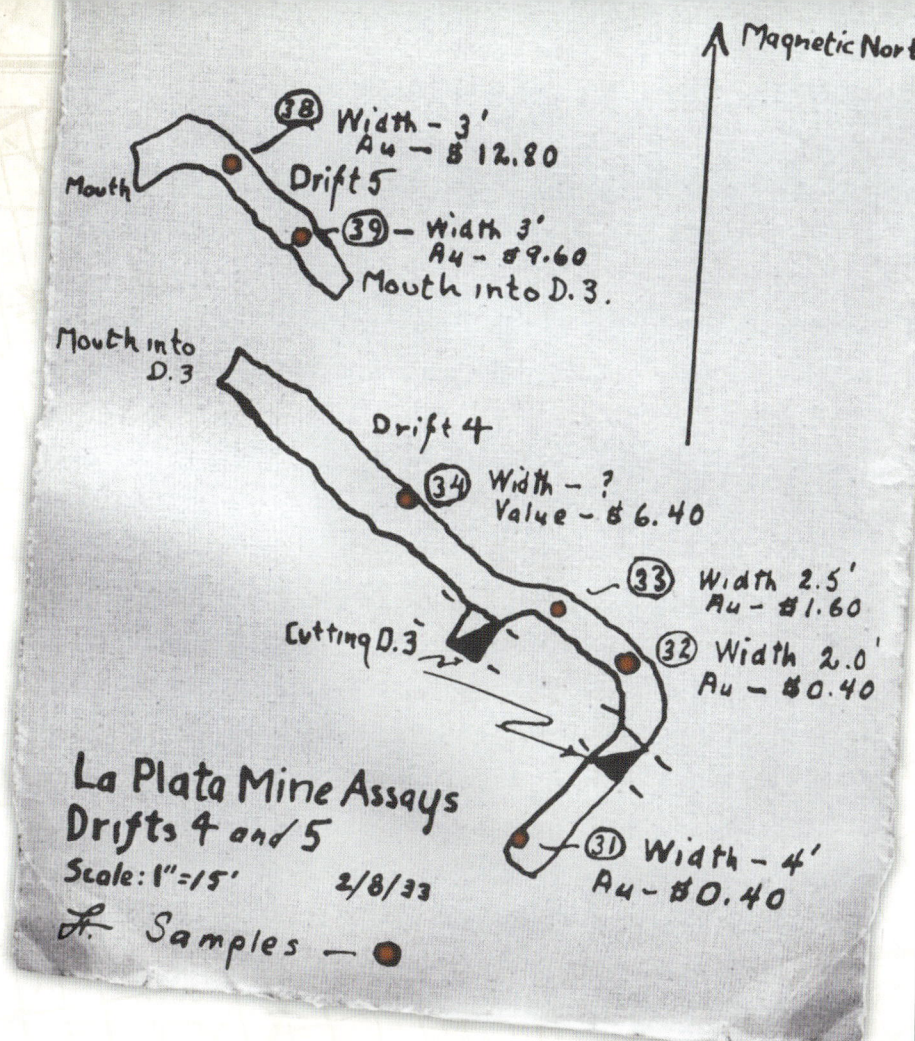

In company with Jose and Martin we inspected the concrete dams—now almost demolished—which Sayer had erected for his sluices, and we heard how rain would invariably drive the river over its banks to sweep away the workings just before any gold could be recovered.

After locating a likely spot, Carper built a test sluice from discarded boards, and we began the task of sluicing the Río Negro in hope of fabulous riches. The sluice itself was a simple affair—a twenty foot box without a top, a foot deep and a foot wide, with riffles inserted at four-inch intervals crosswise down its entire length. The most work associated with this sluice fell on my shoulders, for no one would expect an engineer to stoop to common labor, and the natives were not quite strong enough to play beanbag with four hundred pound gunnysacks. I constructed a long dam across the river by laying these sacks end to end, three high, in such a way that the required amount of water—six inches of drop to every twelve feet of sluice to a depth of seven inches—would flow through our box.

Six natives at fifty cents apiece per day heaved gold-bearing gravel into that box while a gasoline pump kept their pit dry of the water which seeped in from the river.

It was not too much to expect: that we would uncover quantities of gold dust, for on our way to the sluice each morning we passed the famous graveyard of Corozal where alluvial gold exists in abundance. When one dies in the village his only expenses are his priest and coffin, for the grave will be dug in return for the privilege of washing the extracted dirt for gold. And it is claimed that six thousand dollars in nuggets were once found in a single grave.

It was terribly hot and we were soaking wet most of the time, either from a sudden tropical shower or from our own perspiration. I do not know which was the worst for the showers came with such

violence that they left one utterly sodden, and the sweat rolled down the forehead to sting the eyes. During the showers, the natives jumped into the river with all their clothes and swam about, glad for a moment's lull in activities.

Before many days had passed we saw what was meant by a rising river. A twelve foot wall of water marched down upon us leaving us with scant time to swing the sluice box onto the bank. Away went my sandbags, and it was with sinking heart that I recalled the torture of swinging those four hundred pound bags into the rushing stream.

This incident closed our work on the Río Negro, for we had sluiced ten days to a cost of thirty dollars and we had recovered less than fifteen dollars in gold. And that I am told is not good business.

And so Carper, with the little Englishman, scouted about the island in search of newer and better grounds. The Briton was somewhat abashed by our failure as he had stated in writing to his committee that gold was present in that river at an average of three dollars a cubic yard, while we had found it somewhat less than twenty cents.

We moved our sluice to the mid-reaches of the Mavilla River, several miles from Corozal, where Jose Rodriguez claimed to have panned many dollars' worth of dust. And once again we completed the task of building a dam with the proper fall of water and began our labor. But this spot was no more fruitful than the other, and as Carper had left me in charge of the sluice for some days, I closed down shop and paid off the native workers with my last money. After that I sat on my heels and wondered what Carper had found which detained him so long out in the island.

But I did not have to worry for long about Carper and sluicing, as he suddenly took himself and the remainder of the eight hundred dollars out of the picture without even telling me goodbye.

After that I had ample time to study the history of gold mining in Puerto Rico, for I was too broke to do any prospecting other than with a pan, and succor as usual, was terribly slow.

Martin and Jose did their best to console me with tales of great riches, and I learned a little about gold mining. Jose had found employment with most of the prospectors who had come to the district and he told me of the ways they went about their work, how foolish they were, and why they finally failed to become wealthy. Martin had a Spanish chemistry book which had been printed in 1800 and with this as his final court of appeals he set himself up as a competent mining engineer. Whenever I would question some statement of Martin's concerning odd bits of rock, he would pull at his fierce mustachios and produce his reference from the hip pocket of his soiled breeches to prove his point with words which neither he nor I had suspected of the Spanish language.

Both Martin and Jose ostensibly made their living with a gold pan, although I suspect that Jose depended upon the money his daughters brought him from the schoolteaching, and that the coffers of Martin were filled now and then by a well known political group for which he was the Corozal exponent. Gold mining was their sport and hobby, and they could never quite grasp the fact that I was commercially in dead earnest.

It is true that gold dust may be panned on every river in the district, and that there are but few spots which are utterly barren. By panning religiously, a native is able to make upwards to fifty cents a day with his pan, although their average return is considerably less. In lieu of our steel mining pan, they use a wooden bowl shaped like a Canton coolie hat which they term "gaveta." This word in Spanish really means "dresser drawer," and so, I presume, the term is local. The "gaveta" is fashioned

Left
The Puerto Rican interior, where amidst great ferns, thick thorns and entwining underbrush, firm ground proved as illusive as fabled veins of gold; photograph by L. Ron Hubbard

in one piece from the trunk of a large tree, and as large trees are almost extinct on the island, it grows increasingly difficult each year to procure wooden pans. "Gavetas" are easily handled and, under tropical conditions, they are actually more efficient than the steel pan, as the sweat from one's hands is enough to float gold out of the pan and back into the stream. Wood, unlike steel, does not seem to hold the grease on the surface of the water. The natives use a circular, swinging motion, not at all orthodox, but they are able to separate gold and black sand—the panner's enemy—with great ease.

Being bored, lonesome, and broke I found a "gaveta" and attempted to ascertain by experiment the true quantities of alluvial gold in the rivers of Corozal, and by this method to uncover the lode source of all the gold of the region. But wherever I went throughout the area, the amount of gold was dishearteningly constant and refused to point by concentration to any surface source. This was an odd fact and is rather hard to grasp as there must be, by all known laws of geology, a concentration point or a mother lode. But there was not and I was greatly puzzled.

After wearing out my boots within a space of two months I contented myself with listening to stories hoping that my hotel landlady would remember something of her religion when I stalled her off another time.

That hotel really deserves mention. It was a one story structure on the corner of the plaza directly across the street from the jail. The floors were innocent of paint, the windows of glass, the building of silence, but the food was far from innocent of that substance close to the heart of the Spaniard—garlic. The landlady was quite the character of the town—a jolly overweight soul who had worn out two husbands and had divorced a third. But aside from her continual chatter at the top of her voice, she was quite easy on the nerves.

Below
Ron's sluicing pans for extracting alluvial gold from streambeds

My room was directly over a pigsty, and through the cracks in the floor I could view the amiable beasts moving to and fro. My window faced a blank wall three feet away, and my mosquitoes were quite the largest ever seen in the captivity of a mosquito net.

Corozal itself was a boisterous little town which housed five thousand people on the four streets which surrounded the plaza. It was a standard West Indian village with its church in the center of the public square and the sewer system in the middle of the streets. Small though it was it was not without excitement. Western thrillers could be viewed each night at

Above
Small horses and mules replaced vehicles as interior terrain grew increasingly rugged; photograph by L. Ron Hubbard

the cine, drunken Spanish caballeros were forever disputing the police, and at least once a day some major crime would dart forth to amaze the populace. For instance, one day a small boy made off with three of my landlady's pennies, to be led away weeping. It was well that he wept, for he was to spend the next few years in a reformatory.

Spaniards are death on crime and make every provision for its prompt apprehension and punishment. They mete out as much as three months in jail to he who would slay his neighbor in cold blood. And the sentence is usually passed upon the offender for his audacity in carrying a concealed weapon. As the government permit costs thirty-five dollars, the price is above the purse of the hillman, and the majority of them are forced to carry their weapons without the sanction of the law. A seven inch knife is also considered a concealed weapon even when worn in plain sight, though the natives swing their two foot machetes from their belts without molestation.

The jail across the road, in full view of the outside door of my bedroom, created no little amusement. At one time it housed a murderer for his usual three months, and each morning I would awake to the sound of his jolly conversation as he chewed sugar cane on the front steps of the police station and talked politics with his fellow townsmen.

We had a crazy woman, too, who enlivened matters a little when they became too dull by throwing fits in the center of the public square. She was young and exceedingly wild, picking her exhibition time as nine o'clock almost without fail.

One night as I rounded the plaza rather late I encountered the murderer strolling complacently past the church. Around his index finger he swung a key. I was startled and said so, but he explained with a Spanish shrug that they had placed the crazy woman in his cell, that she had annoyed him exceedingly with her songs and screeches and that he had thought it best to lock her in. But his main grievance was that she had robbed him of his lawful place of rest, and that he must stroll about the plaza for the remainder of the night. Next morning, he was back on the steps of the police station chewing his sugar cane and explaining to his audience the latest moves of the Liberal Party.

These people are a mixture of more than five races in varying degrees, and some of the effects are startling. Carib Indians had inhabited the island before the advent of Columbus and had accordingly been graced with not a little Spanish blood. The Spanish had imported Chinese to labor in their mines and fields, and this blood had become entangled with that of the first two. Then came the Africans from the slave ships, and later, the northerner. Now all five are inseparably mingled, creating a new race of their own. All these bloods have gone together to make the "jibaro" or hillman who speaks his own brand of Spanish and who ekes out an existence on less than we pay for our tobacco.

Martin had a habit of looking up a hill and gesticulating wildly "Mucho oro fino," meaning of course, "Much fine gold." And then before I could stop him he would point to a depression in a hillside and describe how the Spaniards chained Caribs, Chinese and Africans together in long lines to make them bring bag after bag of dirt in leather sacks which they were forced to wash in the rivers to recover the precious yellow metal.

Some of Martin's stories about these diggings were interesting, even though they may have strayed far from fact. He explained how the Spanish had acquired Chinese laborers from rulers of South China, how the laborers had been worked hard on the gold diggings and in the fields, and how the Spaniards had avoided the payment of wages to the Chinese potentates. Upon the expiration of the Chinese contracts, according to Martin, the Spaniards marched the Chinese out into the sea and gave the sharks a free dinner, afterwards writing to China that the laborers had all died of fever.

But whatever the Spaniards did, they were certainly thorough and intelligent about their gold work. They seem to have stripped the entire island of whatever gold it might once have had, and I happened upon proof of the fact that they did not content themselves with alluvial gold.

High upon a mountain in the region of Palo Blanco with a sheer hillside dropping off a few thousand feet to a river, there is an old shaft, now nothing but a depression in the peak. And around that depression is a small quantity of rock which is excellent honey-comb quartz. This rock is bejeweled with flecks of pure gold, and though there is not enough of the substance present to allow a commercial realization, the fact remains that the Spaniards had actually done rock mining three centuries or more ago.

It is very difficult to prospect in Puerto Rico. The entire island is a mass of mountains, rugged and sharp, and the underbrush outside the confines of the fields, is almost impenetrable. And it is obvious that a little ledge of rock only a few feet wide is easier seen when not covered, and almost impossible to see when shrouded by dense tropical vegetation. As the island was not cultivated to any extent at the time of Columbus, it is easy to see that in vein mining, the Conquistadores had a colossal task before them.

However, gold mining was almost all they knew, for the customs of the island, most of them still unchanged through four centuries, bear ample evidence of their ignorance of agriculture and industry.

Right
"These people are a mixture of more than five races in varying degrees, and some of the effects are startling"—LRH; photograph by L. Ron Hubbard

Having colonized the West Indies, Spain was hard put to keep them colonized. Of the two types of men who rallied to the islands, only one showed any tendency to remain and finish the task before them. This latter type was, of course, the priest, filled with religious zeal, glorying in the numbers of helpless heathens whose souls he could save. The other type was the true Conquistador who thirsted for gold and adventure and who used the natives as human machines to perform the tasks set for them. The majority of Spaniards were of the Conquistador variety, and when they landed, where they had expected to find heaps of glittering gold awaiting them on the waterfront, they found only lowering mountains in a topsy-turvy country which would divulge its riches only after months, even years, of toil had been spent upon them.

Below
The Palo Blanco, originally mined by Spaniards in the 1600s; photograph by L. Ron Hubbard

Perhaps because of their pasts in Spain, the Conquistadores who landed in Puerto Rico strode into the task of mining their gold. But before much headway could be made with their mines, two things happened. Ponce de León arrived as the first governor of the island, and Pizarro whipped the Incas into furnishing golden cargos for his galleons.

Upon hearing the story of Pizarro, the Spaniards in Puerto Rico snatched up their plumed hats, buckled on their swords, and began to drum up transportation to the mainland. But Ponce de León, cantankerous no doubt over his failure to find his fountain of youth, was determined that his colony would remain populated. And so, before even a handful of his gentlemen could put to sea, the governor ordered the remainder to stay. He caused a new gibbet to be erected and his executioner polished up his ax, and the Conquistadores thought better of their plans and stayed.

Above
The older mines could only be accessed from the end of a dangling rope; photograph by L. Ron Hubbard

Before many years, most of the placer gold had been exploited, the lode gold had been found to be meager, and it was necessary that, to live, these fighting gentlemen of old Castile must turn their Toledo blades into machetes in an effort to wrest their riches from agriculture.

But they evidently knew vastly more about the art of spitting heathens than they did about cutting their crops. They fell back upon the unreliable trial and error method, and the Puerto Rican brand of agriculture, even as it is accomplished today, came into being.

One of the most significant customs which tattle upon the Conquistadores is the manner in which Puerto Rican oxen are yoked. In almost every other country of the world where oxen have ever slaved as beasts of burden their yokes have been securely rested upon their necks just forward of the hump. But not so in Puerto Rico, for even today when men should know better, the Puerto Rican follows the custom set by the Conquistadores and yokes his oxen by the horns. Evidently, the original Spaniards knew no other way. A bit of wood across the end of the tongue of the cart or plow is securely lashed to the horns and every bit of pulled weight falls directly upon the neck instead of the shoulders. In this way only half the amount of work can be done, and Mr. Ox is sure to go to bed with a neck-ache.

Many words I wasted in attempts to uproot this institution, and undo some of the work of the Spaniards, but I was always met by the statement that it was known to be an evil custom, but that, unanswerably, their fathers had done it in that manner.

When the Conquistadores established a custom, the country usually adhered to it. The dress of the Puerto Rican woman of today is identical with those worn in Spain at the time Columbus sailed home to be called a liar. This native dress is almost the same wherever the Conquistador unsheathed his sword. Natives of the South Seas, when they are not wearing a Mother Hubbard in sweaty virtue, wear the same regalia as the Puerto Rican. The costume consists of a short gauze shirtwaist with abbreviated balloon sleeves, pulled down to a high waist over a colorful bodice, and set off by a voluminous skirt which is simply a few yards of cloth draped about the hips. The comb at the back of the brunette head and the gayly colored shawl are woeful in their absence. Incidentally, I have never seen this costume outside of a cabaret which boasted a chorus.

About the time I had come to a conclusion that every bump on every hill in Puerto Rico was a mine dump and that every depression was a placer digging of the 1600s, my friends in the north sent support to me in the form of Thomas Finley McBride of the Butte School of Mines in Montana, who carried a little gold medal which proclaimed him as the most promising graduate of the previous year.

The best thing Mac found that he didn't like was the pernicious *mañana* habit of the natives. During the first week of his advent he determined that one of the reasons he seemed to progress slowly was to be found in his lack of Spanish. Accordingly he set himself to the task of mastering a new language, and it was the short sum of three months before he could finally make himself understood. I deem this record time for the absorption of a new tongue.

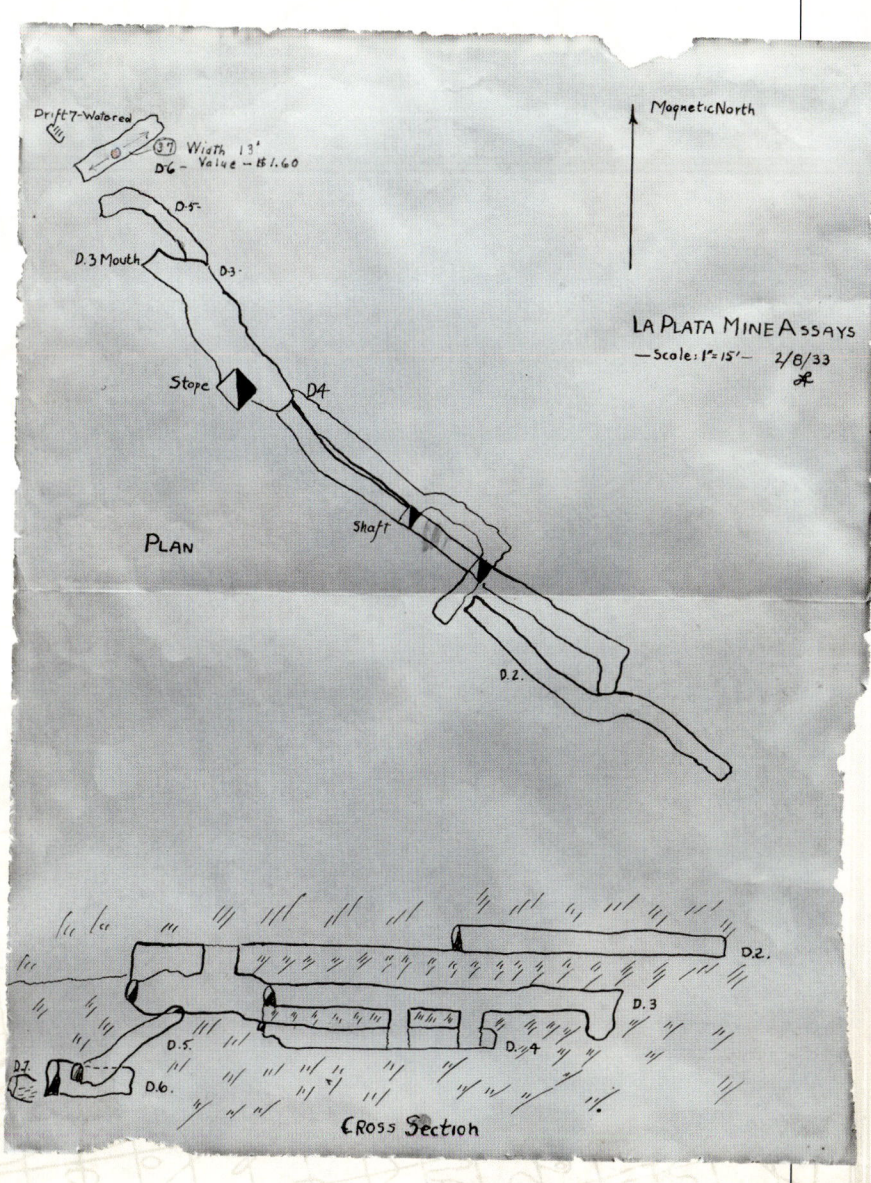

Mac and I searched high and low, out and beyond for ledges of the precious ore, but search though we did, and sweat and curse in Spanish, we finally simmered our prospects down to four.

All of these four diggings were of recent date, but the engineers who had made them all seem to have been lacking in mineralogical savvy, and we based our hopes on the supposed incompetence of our predecessors.

The first was located high in the jungle of El Yunque near the village of Luquillo. The Río Sabana was nearby, and as we had learned that the Conquistadores had panned a great deal of their gold from this stream, we sighed and tackled the jungle.

Four natives with machetes hewed away the giant ferns and entwining underbrush and we slowly worked in toward our goal. I have seen worse in the South Pacific and the Philippines, but I minded this stretch of jungle

particularly because of a horse. For some reason I have still to remember, I had brought a horse on the journey. It was impossible to ride him as he stumbled and lunged through the thick thorn-trees and tripped over long, sturdy vines. Leading him was an adventure in itself as he thought nothing of trodding solidly on my bootheels. At times it was necessary to lift him over fallen logs, one set of feet at a time. Now that may sound a bit weird, but consider the fact that Puerto Rican horses are a vest-pocket edition, weighing only about twice as much as a man.

After long hours of sweaty struggle we reached our objective and inspected the three pitiful dents in a mountain of stone and poisonous thorns. The veins were but a few inches wide and their gangue extremely poor, barely mineralized.

An American Engineer named Morton had made these holes, and it is rumored about San Juan that he committed suicide when it was discovered that he was a spy for the German government in the World War. However, it is Mac's steadfast opinion that the man killed himself from sheer shame of his limited mining knowledge.

This brings to mind the stories which I used to tease Mac. It would seem that to date no mining engineer who invaded Puerto Rico lived to tell the tale, and a fascinating game ensued which had for its object the promise that Mac would never live to return to his Rockies and his girl.

Sayer might be called the first casualty. He spent his fortune and drank himself to death. Then there was Morton in 1914. Trautman, an engineer who had made his fortune from a manganese mine during the World War, found a mountain crowded with gold veins, pushed eight drifts into the stubborn lava. He died in the southern part of the island shortly after he had pauperized himself. A young American was supposed to have discovered a rich vein in the region of Barrio del Carmen a few years ago and one of his tunnels still juts into a hillside. But the story is told that he celebrated shortly after his discovery, insulted a townsman of Carmen, and was buried in the basin. Not far from Carmen another American engineer carelessly stopped three bullets from the gun of a drunken jibaro. The diggings of Peter Nelson are everywhere in evidence over the island, and so was Peter Nelson until he died of fever and an overdose of French brandy. The one mine of note which he discovered is so entangled with stockholders that no one will ever be able to realize a profit from the site.

That might give you the idea that our prospecting careers in Puerto Rico were loaded to the gunwales with blood and thunder. This, however, is not exactly the case, for the only accident which befell us resulted from my indiscreet insistence that I ride a mule.

We had inspected the Barrio del Carmen, the Minillas mine of Trautman at San Germán, and had generally covered the terrain. We were returning once more for a last look at the basin of Carmen which contains a startling number of valueless veins when I suddenly became tired of riding a horse. Most of our horses were worn beasts, but the one I had straddled for two full days was so tight of muscle that it seemed only one more step would be needed to complete my undoing. And so I begged a mule.

That brings up the subject of cinches, and it is with sadness in my voice that I must assure you that the Conquistadores had forgotten to tell the natives that a cinch belongs with a saddle, and down through the four hundred years, a cinch has been a taboo.

I mounted carelessly, placing my full weight in the left stirrup, not knowing that the mule was blind in his left eye. The saddle scurried bellyward, my field boot refused to leave the stirrup, and my right foot, rising, struck the mule a square and personal blow.

When I came to, Pedro Rojas was bending over me moaning that he had no candles or priest and that my soul was certainly purgatory-bound. I uncrossed my precisely folded arms and sat up, thereby scaring Pedro out of three shades of color, to find my ribs in a remarkable second-hand condition.

However, my plight made little difference for our work was done. We had slaved and sweated for months and we had nothing more tangible to show than a mediocre vocabulary of crude hillman Spanish. Of alluvial gold we had found nothing in payable amounts. And veins were plentiful in number but startlingly scarce in gold content.

Thus we packed up and caught the first steamer for home.

Now that, by rights, should end my saga, as one is not supposed to resort to coincidence in stories. But as this is a true yarn, I might as well scour it down and give you the final punch.

Thereafter I settled down to a period of recuperation on my friend's farm in Maryland, and I suppose I would have been recuperating still had it not been for a sudden yearning to shoot at a target.

I cleaned up a twenty-two rifle and we went out into the orchard. But it was difficult to secure the target to a tree, and my friend discovered a rusty nail and handed me a rock. I had struck the nail twice when my friend asked me what gold ore looked like. I gesticulated with the stone in my hand, and mentioned, in an off-hand manner, that gold ore was very similar to the piece of quartz I held in my hand. Then I started to pound the nail once more. But my friend advanced the startling idea that, if gold ore held the same appearance as the rock I held in my hand, why was it that the rock in my hand was not gold ore. I thought that over for a moment and then looked back at the rock.

By blinking my eyes with great rapidity I finally managed to blurt out that it was, without doubt, a piece of gold-bearing quartz.

We went over the surrounding hillside and everywhere we looked, we saw gold ore. Tons and tons of it lying loose on the surface. And then we discovered the outcrops which told the story of a tremendous vein.

Even then we refused to believe it. O. Henry had been dead for years, and such a snap ending was not possible in real life. But nevertheless, there was the wide vein, all within this property, and to place a value on our find, we sent ore to New York for assay.

While we waited for the gold assay to return, I mentioned it casually to one or two of the townsmen of Beallsville, but in a typical Maryland way, they looked at me and then resumed their discussions of corn and farm relief.

The assay finally arrived and ended our suspense by stating that the ore ran $82.47 a ton in gold content with a slight amount of silver.

But here was the supreme joke of our lives. I had walked over this field time after time, seeing nothing, had gone 1,300 miles south to find something which had lain two feet under my shoe soles.

And the moral of this story is: Never go gold prospecting in the West Indies, especially when you have a gold mine in your own back yard.

Left Beallsville, Maryland, farm where Ron made his fateful discovery of a pure gold vein, 1933

LRH by illustrator/portraitist Richard W. Albright

Buried Alive!

*I*NCLUDED IN THE STUFF OF ADVENTURE THAT MARKED RON'S PUERTO RICAN EXPEDITION was a near-fatal collapse of a San Germán mine shaft. Eventually part of the fodder for a celebrated collection of stories appearing in *Argosy* magazine and known as the "Hell Job" series, we present the *Argosy* note on the incident as reported to readers in 1936.

L. Ron Hubbard, author, adventurer, aviator, and ex-Marine, almost lost his life in securing data for his "Hell Job" series of dangerous profession stories now running in *Argosy* weekly.

While inspecting a mine at San Germán, Puerto Rico, he came closer to death than any of his fiction heroes. In order to look over an abandoned mine it was necessary for Hubbard and a native helper to squeeze through a half-caved shaft which was held by rotting timbers. Dirt rattled off the walls and down his neck. Everything was silent except the scratch of hobnails. Then suddenly he felt the timber caving in on him. He threw himself down. The candle went out. He got on his hands and knees pushing his back against the wall trying to keep himself from being buried alive.

Dirt rattled. For agonizing seconds he stood there in the dark waiting to be crushed. No crews were outside to dig him out. With terrific concussion the roof dropped ten feet up the drift. Anxiously he crawled back and forth trying to find a way out. There was none. The timber he had been supporting leaned inward and then dropped, half burying Hubbard and the native. He could barely breathe. He couldn't see. He awaited death that might be days in coming.

More than an hour passed. Finally he heard something scratching. Hobnails on the next level. Hubbard yelled and rescue was then a matter of seconds. There was a stope almost above him. A line was lowered. Anxious natives had worried over Mr. Hubbard's absence and had come investigating.

Says Mr. Hubbard: "That was the closest call I ever want to have. An airplane crash, drowning, the bends, a 'soup' explosion, a fall…these are all swift and sure death, but to lie in a hole in the earth in silence and wait for death…that is something else." ∎

College Park Airfield, Washington, DC, 1933;
photograph by L. Ron Hubbard

CHAPTER TWO

An Introductory Word on "SPINNING IN"

An Introductory Word on
"Spinning In"

More or less on the heels of Asia, a twenty-year-old L. Ron Hubbard called a first fateful meeting of the George Washington University Glider Club. Initially, less than a dozen hearty souls replied, while less still turned up at Congressional Airfield for lessons in a Franklin PS2 glider. Just so, the George Washington University Buzzards were born and Ron had taken to the skies.

It was flying as man was intended to fly, "precariously, and by the seat of your pants," as wits of the day remarked. Instrumentation was crude—an altimeter at best—while crafts were either towed from a bumper or flung from cliffs by means of shock cords. Then, too, let us not forget these were still largely experimental days: Lindbergh had crossed the Atlantic only four years earlier and most of what went aloft was still clothed in dope and fabric secured with piano wire. Nevertheless, sparked by a proliferation of German clubs (where a Treaty of Versailles prohibited power), the glider had inspired much American enthusiasm through the early 1930s. More than a few universities had organized clubs, while many an engineering department proffered new designs. That Franklin PS2, for example, with closed cockpit (as opposed to the primary's open) and yet suitable for both training and soaring, had originally sailed off a campus drawing board. Nor was it only an amateur sport, and even the likes of Lucky Lindy and Frank "Mr. Pilot" Hawks were not above sailing in a powerless ship.

Ron's first ascent was typical. On May 6, 1931, under the tutelage of local instructors Glenn Elliott and Don Hamilton, he secured the Franklin's nose to a Model T Ford—at which point, as he tells it: "The car starts; the rope tightens; there is a cloud of dust where the wingtip dips into the ground." Next followed sixteen runs at an altitude of twenty-five feet, another ten runs at over a hundred, and eleven slow turns at ninety degrees—all while asking: "What sort of mesmerism does a glider exercise that it makes a man eat, sleep, talk and fly

Left The legendary "Flash" Hubbard

Right
As a roving correspondent for *The Sportsman Pilot,* Ron regularly provided commentary and photographs on aerial matters of the day. In this case, a Marine Corps biplane at Maryland air meet, 1933.

until he is on the verge of a breakdown?" To eventually earn the 385th American glider license required another fifteen days of formal instruction and a genuinely demanding Department of Commerce exam. But in any case, he was thereafter regularly seen aloft, "with never a sound but the whisper of wind in your struts and maybe the slap, slap, slap of a helmet strap whipping back up over the leading edge."

Yet make no mistake, it was dangerous. As of 1931, some three hundred souls had fallen to their deaths in powerless ships, while an earlier attempt to launch a primary glider from George Washington University had sent a young man to the hospital. It was not for nothing, then, Ron presents his "Spinning In." By way of incidental background, let us add that Ron's account of a first brush with death in the skies appeared in an aviator's bible known as *The Sportsman Pilot,* for which he regularly supplied articles as a nationally recognized correspondent. Also from such adventures came the fodder for later fiction published in the likes of *Argosy* and *Five-Novels Monthly*. Finally, the Port Huron, Michigan, glider club had been founded by the aforementioned Phil "Flip" Browning of Ron's Caribbean Motion Picture Expedition, and of whom we shall hear more in the article to follow. ∎

SPINNING IN

by L. Ron Hubbard

You've probably heard that soaring is not a sport to be lightly taken. Anybody foolish enough to *look* at a motorless plane cancels his insurance immediately. Ask Dick du Pont or Jack O'Meara.

Or read the rest of this.

I had been doing quite a little flitting about on silent wings, using auto tow—gaining altitude by means of a rope from the back of a car to the nose of your glider and cutting loose when you get two-five-six hundred feet upstairs.

It's all very silent and very spooky, sitting up in the clouds with never a sound but the whisper of wind in your struts and maybe the slap, slap, slap of a helmet strap whipping back up over the leading edge.

I'd gotten a first class rating—Department of Commerce Motorless Aircraft License 385 if you want a verification—and I'd been used to utility gliders which look like a power ship without a motor, having an enclosed cockpit.

Once I had me a neat little thrill when an updraft which roared like ten thousand tigers hit one wing, bopped up the nose when I was almost stalling and threw me over for a full turn from four hundred feet. Coming down I could look straight ahead and count every blade of grass.

Below
Ron's epigrammatic flying cap with the Japanese character for "Good Luck"

In the cockpit of his Franklin PS2 glider: "I told these lads that I would teach them how to fly this thing and they all said that was fine"—LRH

The whole world went in a wide circle like looking straight down on a humming top, rushing up at me hundreds of feet at a bite. I couldn't get the controls to take until I was about thirty feet off. Then I straightened her through some luck, which is still a back debt, and I shot level at about ninety miles an hour—and a soaring plane goes at about twenty in regular flight.

Outside of a couple minor scrapes, this was all that had happened to me out of a couple hundred flights, some of them rather long, upwards to two hours without a motor or an oar, just floating along with the breeze.

And so I thought I was the guy Old Lady Luck had always wanted to favor, and I thought I could get away with most anything.

Being young and foolish, I borrowed me some more time off the old gentleman with the whiskers and took a trip up to Michigan. Port Huron, to be exact.

Up there some lads had organized, eighteen months before my arrival, a glider club. They had a ship but they had made one mistake. Like almost any power pilot will try to tell you, they believed anybody could fly one of those box kites and come out whole. But after two attempts to get off, their nerves failed them and they put the crate in a barn and decided that they were valuable to their wives and children.

And there the crate lay, all covered with dust and hay, with the piano wire rusted half through and the dope cracking on the ancient muslin.

Below
Certification as the 385th US licensed glider pilot

Anybody with half his wits about him would have recognized that it was a flying wooden kimono. But I believed, praising Allah, that my luck was forever good.

I told these lads that I would teach them how to fly this thing for so much per flight and they all said that was fine, but I better see if the thing would fly first as it had *never* been off the ground.

Nothing daunted, we promptly hauled the withered, battered wreck from its comfortable warm hay and assembled it.

It was not the kind of ship I had been used to. It was not one of these sleek, go-to-the-devil demons that flowed through chunks of blue with never a tremble. It was what is known as a primary glider. I had never flown one of them before. It was a leftover from the craze which hit this country from Germany about 1927. None of these ships, I discovered later, could fly, and yet men bought them and said, "One thing about gliding. You don't have to have any instruction." Oh, well, maybe they like pushing daisies, some of those guys.

"Four hundred feet above the earth, I heard a sound something like BBs hitting a bell. I went over to a forty-five degree list instantly. The controls sagged and wouldn't take."

It got about the countryside, that afternoon, that a young feller was going to take that there contraption off and go skittering around in it without no motor. As that was quite impossible, the Sunday joy riders all came out to the clodded field to watch. Some five hundred people were there and, as I was never known for modesty, I got me a boy with a Model A Ford and told him how to tow gliders.

He took off in his car, but the glider stayed down. The wind was blowing about thirty miles and the next try he tried it at forty-five in spite of screaming springs.

Fine, I got off that time. Straight flight, although the controls were soggy, and all was well. The next flight I got up to about two hundred feet and landed straight on into the wind again. Fine. Now I'd see what the lousy piece of junk would do. I'd try a full turn, downwind, at four hundred feet.

Now I must explain that this primary didn't have a cockpit. You sat out on a thin board and you could see earth between your knees. Your feet were strapped to the rudders and a safety belt held you against the frame. You were all out in the open, completely unprotected, with wires running out in every direction from you.

I got away with the next several turns and all was well. The thing had a flying speed of wind plus car, or about seventy-five miles an hour—three times too fast exactly.

Then came the last flight that sky surfboard would ever make. I got the full stretch of the rope and cut loose. The ship bounced up, free and bucking like a bronc. I whipped the nose down and it came up again. Four hundred feet above the earth, I heard a sound something like BBs hitting a bell.

I went over to a forty-five degree list instantly. The controls sagged and wouldn't take. Four hundred cold hard feet below was the earth—almost four-fifths of the way up the Washington Monument.

And me with no control over this crazy steed. The wings were folded up, the flying wires, already rusty, could not have stood the strain of that last lurch. No wings, and almost an angel.

The nose, because I was the weight there, went suddenly down. The ship changed into an aerial bomb, using me for the fragmentation. I was about to be exploded over several acres of Michigan cow pasture. I'd hit, strapped there as I was, unable even to withdraw my feet, and then the whole plane would be a mallet to drive me into the ground. Ugh!

Spinning In 61

Above
A Franklin PS2 glider in tow and (hopefully) bound for the skies

Gathering speed, the plane and I began to whistle. The earth was still a long, long ways away. I became impatient. Here I was falling at it, accelerating according to Newton's law 32.2 feet per second, and I wasn't going anywhere at sixty miles or better per straight down.

The world tipped and swayed like a catcher's mitt trying to palm me, the ball. White faces were turned up at me and I could look right down their throats. But I wouldn't hit them. No, I told myself, that was swell. I would hit the only spot below which wasn't moving—the center of two car tracks, nice and hard.

About this time I couldn't do much breathing I was going so fast. That worried me quite a bit, as if it really mattered.

What a long ways down it was!

I cautiously felt those useless controls. The elevators were still working and I amused myself by wiggling them. If I went fast enough, maybe I could pull the old baby out of it a split instant before I hit. Maybe I could save me a broken neck after all.

Sitting up—or rather horizontal, seeing that I faced straight down—I tried this again. I could actually level her out if I wanted, at the last instant. Fine!

And the ground was still coming up, up, up and I could have classified every wildflower under me, I could see them so sharply. Wildflowers when I was about to hit about three times the speed of an express train, streamlined.

Suddenly I knew it wasn't any use. Too many people were looking straight up. Two kids, about ten, wanted to get a better idea of this from below. Before I could yell—it was all so silent I could hear the gasps—these two youngsters were right where I would hit *if* I pulled her level the last instant. A lot of plane poundage would smash them flat.

Oh, dear no. I had to let her hit and hit damned hard and that would be the end of soaring pilot 385.

I heard somebody yell in surprise, "Hot dawg!"

It was me. That's all I had to say about dying.

The last ten feet were there and gone and there came a sound about me like a smashed paper bag and pieces of glider went all over the terrain.

Out? No, I knew all about it in pained surprise. Both my hips were out of joint and I couldn't move. My arms—ye Gods, they must be gone or smashed. I couldn't move them either. I couldn't even raise my head and everything was going blacker and blacker.

Bleeding to death, I told myself bleakly. Hell of a way to die, bleeding to death.

People rallied at last and I heard them yelling foolish things all around the splinters, but I couldn't yell back.

Below
Ron's record of glider flights, including the September 8 entry on which this article is based

Then I heard something going snip, snip, snip. Hands grabbed me and somebody laid me out and I felt my hip joints pop back into place. And then somebody else shoved something between my teeth and strangled me with fire.

I sat up and they say I said, "Well, I got down."

It's a matter of luck I guess, that I did all in one piece that way. Couple ribs broken, a kneecap split, but otherwise so fine and hearty that I went barnstorming the next day and flew constantly for the next six weeks, so it couldn't have been so serious.

But the riddle of why I wasn't killed will never be solved. Unless it was the piano wire. You see, there were yards of the stuff stretching out from me in every direction, and when I hit, the stuff snapped at the other end and, recoiling, wound me up around and around and around like notes through the horn until I couldn't move or breathe or see. I felt the effects of that whipping and I never want to be flogged. Never again, that is.

Maybe I got out because I said, "Hot dawg." I dunno. *Ron*

Right
A pilot who flew as men were intended to fly: "precariously and by the seat of your pants"

Photograph by L. Ron Hubbard

CHAPTER THREE

An Introductory Word on
"TAILWIND WILLIES"

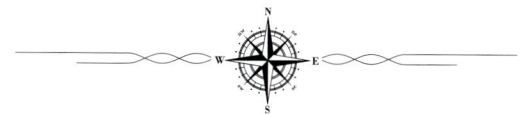

An Introductory Word on "Tailwind Willies"

"COUPLE RIBS BROKEN, A KNEECAP SPLIT, BUT otherwise so fine and hearty that I went barnstorming the next day..."

In fact, L. Ron Hubbard's barnstorming trek had been just such a spontaneous adventure. Fellow aviator Philip Browning had just acquired his LeBlond-powered Arrow Sport (black fuselage, orange wings). Ron had just logged a thirty-minute motorized flight above Michigan and, on September 9, 1931, "with the wind as our only compass," they departed for parts undetermined. To this, and what Ron himself will provide in his "Tailwind Willies," let us add the following:

It was the aerial knight of the First World War who gave impetus to the barnstorming craze, and more than a few claimed previous service with the Lafayette Escadrille or Eddie Rickenbacker's 94th Aero Pursuit Squadron. In any case, surplus war/observation planes were cheap, and many an otherwise unemployed pilot took to the skies to amaze rural townsfolk with breath-catching stunts (and, more lucratively, offer rides for a nominal cost). Although no longer a novelty, Ron and Flip's Arrow Sport adventure engendered the same sort of amazement. Yet there was another side to that Arrow Sport jaunt, and it is important. In what amounts to a companion article entitled "Won't You Sit Down?" and likewise first published in *The Sportsman Pilot,* Ron reports on the state of several private airstrips. If his treatment of the matter is jocular, the subject was not:

"Pick out any strip of country at random and pick out any airport which isn't in general knowledge. You'll read that it has day-and-night service, mechanics, gassing facilities, storage space, and weather information. If you're good at subtraction, follow through on the following: Take away the night service, deduct the weather information, forget about the gas, and mark the storage up to a typographical error. Then if you'll also take away the day service, you'll have a pretty fair picture of Umpteen Airport located

"And they say romance is dead!"—LRH

Right
San Diego Airport and yet another beckoning vision of adventure when flight was young; photograph by L. Ron Hubbard, 1934

in Podunk." His point: The risks of flight were grave enough without factoring in a sodden vegetable patch amidst high-tension wires and calling it an airstrip. In reply came his summary report to the United States Department of Commerce and, by turns, the closing of those strips deemed most unsafe. Yet how he fared along those strips, how it was "to feel a stick under my fingers, feel the ship buck a little under me, see the landscape go sliding by far below, land in stray cornfields under alien suns..."—this is the stuff of "Tailwind Willies." ∎

TAILWIND WILLIES

by L. Ron Hubbard

Last August, my friend Phil Browning (otherwise "Flip") and I found that we had three weeks' excess time on our hands before we had to get back to the college grind. Our resources were one Arrow Sport biplane (companion cockpit, sixty-horse LeBlond), two toothbrushes and four itchy feet. We had accomplished the old stunt of rattling around the country in a Model T in search of adventure, and after a few hours' cogitation, decided that we had a new idea on an old plot. We carefully wrapped our "baggage," threw the fire extinguisher out to save half a horsepower, patched a hole in the upper wing, and started off to skim over four or five States with the wind as our only compass. We had no idea of what we would encounter, but we knew that our "Model T" plane would get us out of whatever we got into, and there we rested content.

Our primary thought had been to get away from people, but we reckoned without the kindly curiosity of the Middle West. Our very first landing in the southern part of Michigan assured us that we belonged to the curio section. We had spotted a nice green meadow, and as the LeBlond had begun to drum too incessantly upon our ears, we landed to obtain some relaxation and a quantity of quiet. We rated neither. Almost before our gear touched the grass, we were surrounded by an anxious crowd which wanted to know whether or not we were still alive. There ensued an hour of continuous caution concerning the prop, and an hour's effort to keep alien feet off the catwalk.

Aviation had become commonplace to our locale, so we found it hard to understand all this curiosity, this abundance of questions. Flip tired himself out explaining all the functions of the parts, and finally in self-defense, we cranked up and continued our journey, resigned to the truth that, after all, aviation was still a sideshow to some people.

Left In the words of an Ohio farm boy: "Them's what we called *Dare Devils!*"

JANUARY, 1932

Tailwind Willies

L. Ron Hubbard

In which the author avows that a pony Pegasus is still a curiosity and hinterland hospitality has survived the Farm Board

LAST August, my friend Phil Browning (otherwise "Flip") and I found that we had three weeks' excess time on our hands before we had to get back to the college grind. Our resources were one Arrow Sport biplane (companion cockpit, sixty-horse LeBlond), two toothbrushes and four itchy feet. We had accomplished the old stunt of rattling around the country in a Model T in search of adventure, and after a few hours' cogitation, decided that we had a new idea on an old plot. We carefully wrapped our "baggage," threw a fire extinguisher out to save half a horsepower, patched a hole in the upper wing, and started off to skim over four or five States with the wind as our only compass.

We had no idea of what we would encounter, but we knew that our "Model T" plane would get us out of whatever we got into, and there we rested content.

Our primary thought had been to get away from people, but we reckoned without the friendly curiosity of the Middle West. Our very first landing in the southern part of Michigan assured us that we belonged in the curio section. We had spotted a likely-looking meadow, and as the LeBlond had begun to drum too incessantly upon our ears, we landed to obtain some relaxation and a quantity of quiet. We rated action almost before our gear touched the ground. We were surrounded by an anxious mob which wanted to know whether or not we were still alive. There ensued about a continuous caution concerning nearly an hour's effort to keep alien feet off catwalk.

Having become commonplace to ourselves, we found it hard to understand this curiosity, this abundance of help. Flip tired himself out explaining the functions of the parts, and in self-defense, we cranked up and took off. Finney, resigned to the truth that aviation was still a sideshow for three weeks, all the rest we did was upstairs in the little Arrow. Our time on terra firma was spent in guarding our ship against thoughtless damage. The grain fields really flew, and we had to "make ourselves

right at home." Hospitality was proffered in all its forms, and if anyone thinks that this modern machine age has deadened our American kindliness and good fellowship, just let them take a backyard tour of the Middle West. We spent only one night in a hotel, and that because we landed in a thunderstorm after dark. The food offered would have done credit to the Waldorf.

Flip and Ron (left) solemnly set to seek rest upstairs in the office of the "Sparrow"

AT the beginning of the trip we were a little skeptical of our ship's abilities, but when, time after time, she pulled us out of small, muddy fields, we rested assured that the orange wings and wide-spanned wheels were capable of anything. Her faculty for groundlooping at sixty miles an hour saved us from caressing many a fence. Though she climbed slowly when once in the air, she lost very little time whenever we zoomed her out of cornfields to miss trees.

At Newport, Indiana, we landed to take on gas, but the second our wheels touched the grass, we sunk a foot and stopped without rolling twenty feet. We fully expected to nose over, but the *Sparrow* set her teeth and put her tail right down. We took on the gas—only five gallons, to save weight—and then used up half the fuel attempting to get off. Although the field was a mile long, we spanked grass the entire length without rising an inch. The prop almost completed the harvest by chopping at the tall growth and making the sound of a machinegun quartet.

At last we gave up. I crawled out to let Flip take a whirl at it alone. By using up half the field, he managed to wish the muddy *Sparrow* into her element, and after

building some altitude, wheeled over the place where I stood and called down that there was another field a short distance away. After pacifying a sheriff, who was about to lock me up for trespassing, by shoving him into a mud puddle, I hopped onto the running board of a Purdue boy's car and burned road over to Flip's new landing place—if you could call it that.

The second field was little better than the first, and three attempts were necessary before we willed the *Sparrow* up just in time to see a nine-foot telephone wire at the height of our prop. Flip threw the nose down and the wires were a scant foot above my head.

We had intended to leave this section of the country for keeps; but a thunderstorm was all around us, we were almost out of gas, the mags weren't functioning right, and it was almost dark, so we hit dirt again five miles away to stop dead in the middle of a wet plowed field.

After that performance we left southern Indiana for more stout-souled fliers, and picked up the thread of adventure in Kentland, where a county fair was progressing nicely without our help. We tried to buy all the watermelons in Indiana by confining our menu to that fruit for dinner, breakfast and lunch. Some of the grifters showed us around, and that night after the midway darkened we were involved in a minor auto wreck. While the car was being repaired in a garage, Flip and I tried our best to "borrow" the siren of the V. F. D. engine which

For the next two weeks, all the rest we received was found upstairs in the little companion "office." Our time on terra firma was mostly spent in guarding our precious *Sparrow* from thoughtless damage, explaining why airplanes really flew, and refusing invitations to "make ourselves right at home." Hospitality was proffered in all its forms, and if anyone thinks that this modern machine age has deadened our American kindliness and good fellowship, just let them take a backyard tour of the Middle West. We spent only one night in a hotel, and that because we landed in a thunderstorm after dark. The food offered would have done credit to the Waldorf.

"We had no idea of what we would encounter, but we knew that our 'Model T' plane would get us out of whatever we got into..."

At the beginning of the trip we were a little skeptical of our ship's abilities, but when, time after time, she pulled us out of small, muddy fields, we rested assured that the orange wings and wide-spanned wheels were capable of anything. Her faculty for groundlooping at sixty miles an hour saved us from caressing many a fence. Though she climbed slowly when once in the air, she lost very little time whenever we zoomed her out of cornfields to miss trees.

At Newport, Indiana, we landed to take on gas, but the second our wheels touched the grass, we sunk a foot and stopped without rolling twenty feet. We fully expected to nose over, but the *Sparrow* set her teeth and put her tail right down. We took on the gas—only five gallons, to save weight—and then used up half the fuel attempting to get off. Although the field was a mile long, we spanked grass the entire length without rising an inch. The prop almost completed the harvest by chopping at the tall growth and making the sound of a machine gun quartet.

At last we gave up. I crawled out to let Flip take a whirl at it alone. By using up half the field, he managed to wish the muddy *Sparrow* into her element, and after building some altitude, wheeled over the place where I stood and called down that there was another field a short distance away. After pacifying a sheriff, who was about to lock me up for trespassing, by shoving him into a mud puddle, I hopped onto the running board of a Purdue boy's car and burned road over to Flip's new landing place—if you could call it that.

The second field was little better than the first, and three attempts were necessary before we willed the *Sparrow* up just in time to see a nine-foot telephone wire at the height of our prop. Flip threw the nose down and the wires were a scant foot above my head.

We had intended to leave this section of the country for keeps; but a thunderstorm was all around us, we were almost out of gas, the mags weren't functioning right, and it was almost dark, so we hit dirt again five miles away to stop dead in the middle of a wet plowed field.

After that performance we left southern Indiana for more stout-souled fliers, and picked up the thread of adventure in Kentland, where a county fair was progressing nicely without our help. We tried to buy all the watermelons in Indiana by confining our menu to that fruit for dinner, breakfast and lunch. Some of the grifters showed us around, and that night after the midway darkened we were involved in a minor auto wreck. While the car was being repaired in a garage, Flip and I tried our best to "borrow" the siren of the V. F. D. engine which was housed in the same garage. We were unsuccessful, however, and the forthcoming towns were spared the terrors of screeches issuing from the blue. In Ohio, we dropped a pushrod over a solid, if small, field and were lucky enough to find a

Left
College Park Airfield: home of the Washington Barnstormers; photograph by L. Ron Hubbard, 1933

Tailwind Willies

machine shop close by in the town of New London. We spent the night as the guests of a gentleman farmer, the son of a famous professor, whose house was pleasantly cluttered with all manner of things Chinese. That morning had found us trying the only piece of navigation we attempted on the trip, and the results were marvelous. When we were forced down near New London, we found that we were only twenty-seven miles off a fifty-mile course.

Almost every flier has heard that cows love to eat the dope off the wings and even the fabric. Flip and I had put that fact down as just another one of aviation's tall stories. At Andersonville (I forget the State)—whence we had flown in search of beer, which we didn't find and wouldn't have wanted, anyhow—we floated too far and when we landed we groundlooped too fast in avoiding a fence. One tire blew. While we were pumping it up, the other went down. Then the first refused to stay inflated, and evening found us marooned in a cow pasture. A farmer let several cows into the field, and though the cows had never seen a plane before, they dashed up and began to lick the fabric in ecstasy. We spent the next few minutes trying to keep them off until the puzzled farmer came and took them away again. After this we are going to keep the tongue away from the cheek around the hangars.

Top left
Route of the Arrow Sport

Bottom left
Ron's pilot log, officially recording not only his tri-state barnstorming adventure, but also his first official solo flight of August 30, 1931

A renowned aerial photographer, Ron was not unknown to actually shoot from the wing while airborne

One scene we witnessed will remain in my memory a long, long time. It was evening and the sun had almost vanished over the rim. Clouds were all around us on the horizon, their uppermost rifts so level that they made a continuous, circular black curtain which, though miles away, seemed to frown at us as they gradually came closer. We were flying at 3,000 feet, and though we traveled at ninety miles an hour, we seemed to have paused with the rest of an eerie world. Down below, the ground was streaked with long shadows made by trees and houses, small on a rolling terrain. Above the clouds, starting from a sharply defined line, the sky was a magnificent blue, dotted here and there by faint golden stars. For an hour we roared on, the LeBlond seemingly puny in all this expanse.

"We had been up there in all that terrible grandeur so long that we had almoſt ceased to be earthly beings."

Finally, I looked in back of us, and there above that black curtain, reared three flaming red tufts which seemed to blaze. I nudged Flip. He stared back at the clouds and began an immediate search for a landing field. Too much was too much. We had been up there in all that terrible grandeur so long that we had almost ceased to be earthly beings. We circled and circled over a huge stubble field trying to get back to earth. Finally our sense of dimension returned, and we set the *Sparrow* down. Anyway, with all our mishaps, we proved three or four things (something always must be proved by a flight): Light planes are practical for cross-country work; a pilot doesn't have to follow the air lanes and empty his purse into hangar fees—he can get along just as well trying this backyard stunt; and touring for pleasure in a plane is not half as dangerous as the skeptics like to believe, and twice as much fun as any other way.

Sportsmen pilots do not have to limit their flying to their own backyards. The more the U.S. is informally toured, the quicker aviation will find a place in the hearts of the chaps on the byroads. And they say romance is dead!

Right
Hell Raisers of the Skies: Ron "Flash" Hubbard and Philip "Flip" Browning, Washington, DC, 1931

"Flash" Hubbard

With the landing of the Arrow Sport in the autumn of 1931, Ron primarily returned to powerless ships—to that Franklin PS2 at the Congressional Airfield and equally innovative secondary gliders at Detroit fields. Then again, he returned to reporting on flight in ways which likewise placed him on the cutting edge. For example, among other LRH articles to appear in *The Sportsman Pilot* was a then definitive look at experimental radio navigation aptly entitled "Music with Your Navigation," and foretelling of his own adventurous foray into the field with his 1940 Alaskan Radio Experimental Expedition. Also for that publication was his 1934 examination of the fully aluminum Ryan ST (Sport Trainer), brainchild of a legendary T. Claude Ryan, who will forever live in the annals of aviation for his design of Lindbergh's *Spirit of St. Louis*. Finally, there was Ron's genuinely decisive work on Capitol Hill towards the formation of an independent United States Air Force (as opposed to a dependent Army Air Corps) and all other incidental adventures cited here. Providing a keen glimpse of the Ron "Flash" Hubbard as the world of aviation saw him is the following from aviation columnist H. Latane Lewis II. It appeared in *The Pilot* magazine, July 1934.

Whenever two or three pilots are gathered together around the Nation's Capital, whether it be a Congressional hearing or just in the back of some hangar, you'll probably hear the name of Ron Hubbard mentioned, accompanied by such adjectives as "crazy," "wild," and "dizzy." For the flaming-haired pilot hit the city like a tornado a few years ago and made women scream and strong men weep by his aerial antics. He just dared the ground to come up and hit him.

In the beginning, Ron (also known as "Flash") hailed from out west, but only stayed long enough to be born. Since then he has been a dweller of the world at large, and there are few nooks and corners of the earth that he hasn't poked into. Before he fell from grace and became an aviator, he was, at various times, top sergeant in the Marines, radio crooner, newspaper reporter, gold miner in the West Indies, and movie director-explorer, having led a motion picture expedition into the south seas aboard an ancient windjammer.

Then he turned to glider flying. And that is what gave Washington its biggest thrill, for Ron could do more stunts in a sailplane than most pilots can in a pursuit job. He would come out of spins at an altitude of thirty inches and thumb his nose at the undertakers who used to come out to the field and titter.

Once he took a glider up at a Chicago airport which was surrounded by a concrete road. It was a hot day and waves of heat were rising off the road as if it had been a stove. Ron sat on that up current of air and stayed

Aeronautical gentlemen from the George Washington University flying club (L. Ron Hubbard far left), 1931

there. Round and round the airport he went like a merry-go-round, until everybody got dizzy from watching him. Finally, he got tired of chasing his tail and came down, after establishing something of a record for sustained flight over the same field.

Then, one day he got fed up with gliders and decided to try something with power. So he climbed into a fast ship and, without any dual time at all, gave the engine the soup and hopped off. Well, he got back on the ground with the plane still all in one piece and, going on the theory that it's a good landing if you can walk away from it, he realized that he was now a pilot.

Fired by his new prowess, he immediately started barnstorming and ensnared many an unsuspecting passenger. He flew under every telephone wire in the Middle West and cows and horses in that section still shy at the sound of an airplane motor.

After being one of aviation's most distinguished hell raisers, he finally settled down with great dignity and became director of the flying club at George Washington University.

At present, our young hero is buzzing around on the West Coast, where he writes magazine stories between flights. He is now recognized as one of the outstanding glider pilots in the country. ∎

Right top "The flaming-haired pilot hit the city like a tornado…"
Right bottom "Then, one day he got fed up with gliders and decided to try something with power"—aviation columnist H. Latane Lewis II

Who's Who

By H. LATANE LEWIS II

RON HUBBARD

Whenever two or three pilots are gathered together around the Nation's Capital, whether it be a Congressional hearing or just in the back of some hangar, you'll probably hear the name of Ron Hubbard mentioned, accompanied by such adjectives as "crazy," "wild," and "dizzy." For the flaming-haired pilot hit the city like a tornado a few years ago and made women scream and strong men weep by his aerial antics. He just dared the ground to come up and hit him.

In the beginning, Ron (also known as "Flash") hailed from out west, but only stayed long enough to be born. Since then he has been a dweller of the world at large, and there are few nooks and corners of the earth that he hasn't poked into. Before he fell from grace and became an aviator, he was, at various times, top sergeant in the Marines, radio crooner, news-

RON HUBBARD

paper reporter, gold miner in the We... Indies, and movie director... having led a motion picture... into the south seas aboard... windjammer.

Then he turned to gl... And that is what gave... its biggest thrill, for Ro... more stunts in a sailpla... pilots can in a pursuit j... come out of spins at a... thirty inches and thumb... the undertakers who use... to the field and titter.

Once he took a glide... go airport which w... a concrete road. It... waves of heat we... d as if it had been... hat up current of... . Round and r... ent like a merr... ody got dizzy... nally, he got tired of chasing... nd came down, after establish-... hing of a record for sustained... the same fiel...

Then, one day he got fed up with gliders and decided to try something with power. So he climbed into a fast ship and, without any dual time at all, gave the engine the soup and hopped off. Well, he got back on the ground with the plane still all in one piece and, going on the theory that its a good landing if you can walk away from it, he realized that he was now a pilot.

Fired by his new prowess, he immediately started barnstorming and ensnared many an unsuspecting passenger. He flew under every telephone wire in the Middle West and cows and horses of that section still shy at the sound of an airplane motor.

After being one of aviation's most distinguished hell-raisers, he finally...

When he had earned his half wing, he went out to the front with the 12th Aero Squadron and was in the thick of the fighting from June, 1918 until the Armistice.

Wright was a handsome, virtuous-looking lad in those days, and it is hard to believe that any Hun would have been hard-hearted enough to have shot at him if he could have seen his face. But at that time flyers dressed like deep sea divers, and there was no chance for an eye-to-eye encounter. Wright came home with the Distinguished Service Cross, the Croix de Guerre, and the Belgian Order of the Crown dangling from his chest.

The flight that won him the D.S.C. took place during the first two hours of the Argonne offensive. One of the ...ugles of the war was...

CHAPTER FOUR

The "HELL JOB" SERIES

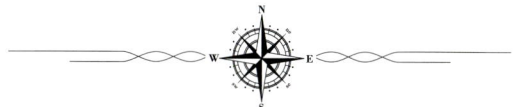

The "Hell Job" Series

QUITE APART FROM ADVENTURE FOR THE SAKE OF adventure, those familiar with the literary works of L. Ron Hubbard may recognize the substance of events recounted here in stories of the 1930s and early 1940s. For example, it was precisely from his Caribbean Motion Picture Expedition that he drew the atmosphere for his *Murder at Pirate Castle,* and thus his scripting of the Columbia Pictures serial based upon that story, *The Secret of Treasure Island*. Similarly, those familiar with Ron's 1936 *Test Pilot,* describing thoroughly accurate aeronautical feats, may have rightly surmised the story had been based on his own feats in the world of aviation. Finally—and here we come to the point—if he lacked the personal experience from which to shape a story, he promptly went out and gained that experience.

Such was the premise of Ron's 1936 "Hell Job" series for *Argosy* magazine (most recently available in the L. Ron Hubbard *Classic Fiction Series*). Having procured a list of "extrahazardous professions," Ron proceeded to pilot experimental aircraft, drive logs down North Pacific rivers, enter wild animal cages and otherwise immerse himself

Below Tales from L. Ron Hubbard's "Hell Job" series as originally published in *Argosy* between 1936 and 1937

Left A few of the world's most dangerous professions and thus jobs deemed too dangerous to underwrite for accident insurance

in the so-called "K jobs," i.e., those deemed too dangerous to underwrite.

As he explains: *"These are the accident taboos. The rating, as you know, starts at A, the preferred risk on accident. This covers clerks and writers and such. Then there is B, a little higher and having more risk to it, and then you go up letter by letter until you get to E. E is just about as high as a company wants to write. The rates are very high. Anything following comes under the head of special policy. F, G, H, I, and J are the upward limits. J is pretty bad, carrying only day to day insurance in most cases and costing as high as fifty percent.*

"Then comes this rating K. K is out completely. It's the ban. They list K's so that they can be certain a K will never come into the office. They don't want to see any of our K's at all. They almost have signs on the door telling them to beat it."

Presented here, in a similarly offhand letter to *Argosy* readers (in the "Argonotes" column), is Ron's description of that "Hell Job" series and particularly as pertaining to his December 1936, *The Shooter*. Drawn from experiences in and around the wildcat fields of Texas, the story concerns some thoroughly rousing adventures of one Mike McGraw: "shooter" of wells, foiler of claim-jumping hoodlums and general roustabout. As a further explanatory note, *soup* is the shooter's term for nitroglycerin, and every bit as temperamental as Ron suggests. The seaside dock from which he plunged actually lay above a very chilled and dark Puget Sound. ∎

Argonotes
The Readers' Viewpoint

by L. Ron Hubbard

This series will either be the making or the ruination of me. Lately I've been following your Argonotes, in which several gentlemen have taken several of us poor writers for a ride. I anticipate a lot of copy for that section with these hazardous occupation stories judging from the diversity of opinions I have received in collecting the material. For instance, two loggers I was talking to last month almost came to blows over the right name for the lad who strings cables in the lumber camps. One claimed it was "high-rigger," the other, "high-faller." According to location, I suppose.

Mining is another thing that varies to beat the devil. All depends upon district, whether coal or metal mining, whether you are a miner or a mining engineer.

Oil wells are the most variable thing in the lot. Every section of the world has a different nomenclature, different methods. I took Texas because I'm familiar with their methods there, but ten to one some roughneck in California is going to pop up with vast objections.

So, I anticipate lots of fun. All along I've realized the score on this and so I have checked and rechecked the data contained in the stories, and I think I've got an airtight answer for every possible squawk.

Something else has amused me considerably. Writers, treating the same subject time after time in fiction, gradually

evolve a terminology and a pattern for certain types of stories as you well know. This creates an erroneous belief in readers that they are familiar with a certain subject through reading so much fiction dealing with it. I've had to shed a lot of that for the sake of accuracy and I'm very, very anxious to have my hand called on some of it. Oil well stories, for instance, always seem to have a villain who, in the height of hate, drops a wrench or something down a well to ruin it. Dropping things into the hole is common. In cable tool drilling, so many hours or days are regularly estimated in with the rest of the work for fishing. The tools fall in, wrenches drop, bits stick, cables break, and wells are never, never abandoned because of it, or is it considered at all serious.

In the oil well story Mike McGraw gnaws upon a lighted cigar while he mixes nitroglycerin. He shoots fulminate caps with a slingshot to explode them. He is, in short, doing everything a man shouldn't do—according to popular opinion. There'll be fireworks in that quarter. Plenty of fireworks. But I've nailed the answers down. Soup, unless confined, will burn slowly when ignited. Smoking while making it is no more dangerous than smoking in a gasoline station—and everybody does that. As for caps, they explode only when they are scratched with steel or when they have been hammered hard. I almost went crazy in Puerto Rico while surveying a metal mine. The native in charge of dynamite was very, very careless, so I thought. One

day, after he had blown a series along a drift, I told him what I thought about it. He was smoking and carrying 60% dynamite at the same time. To my horror he shoved the lighted end of his cigar against a stick. It burned no faster than a pitchy piece of kindling. He used to shoot dogs with fulminate triple-force caps.

The process of digging up data is interesting when I can get these gentlemen to give me a hand. The navy diver here is responsible for the data and authenticity of this story. Going down off the end of a dock didn't give me such a good idea of what it was all about after all. Never got so scared before in all my life. Something ghastly about it. And the helmet is enough to deafen you and the cuffs were so tight my hands got blue.

But it was lots of fun!

When these stories start to come out and when the letters start to come in calling me seven different kinds of a liar (which they will), sit easy and grin and shoot them this way. There isn't anything reasonable in the way of criticism I can't answer anent this collected data.

It was either bow to popular fallacy and avoid all technical descriptions, or ride roughshod, make sure I was right and damn the torpedoes. Making the latter choice, I've laid myself wide open several times to crank letters. So be it.

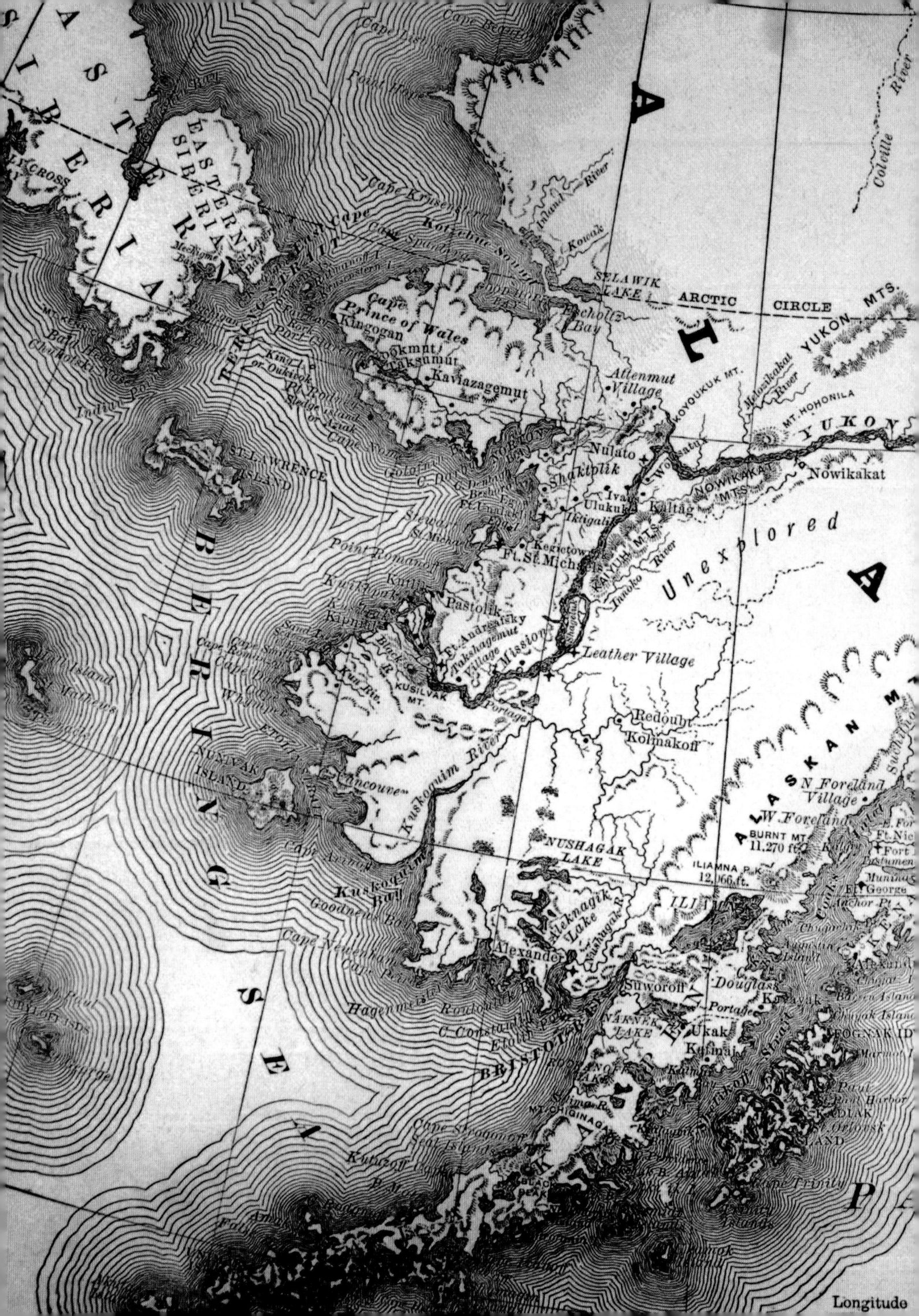

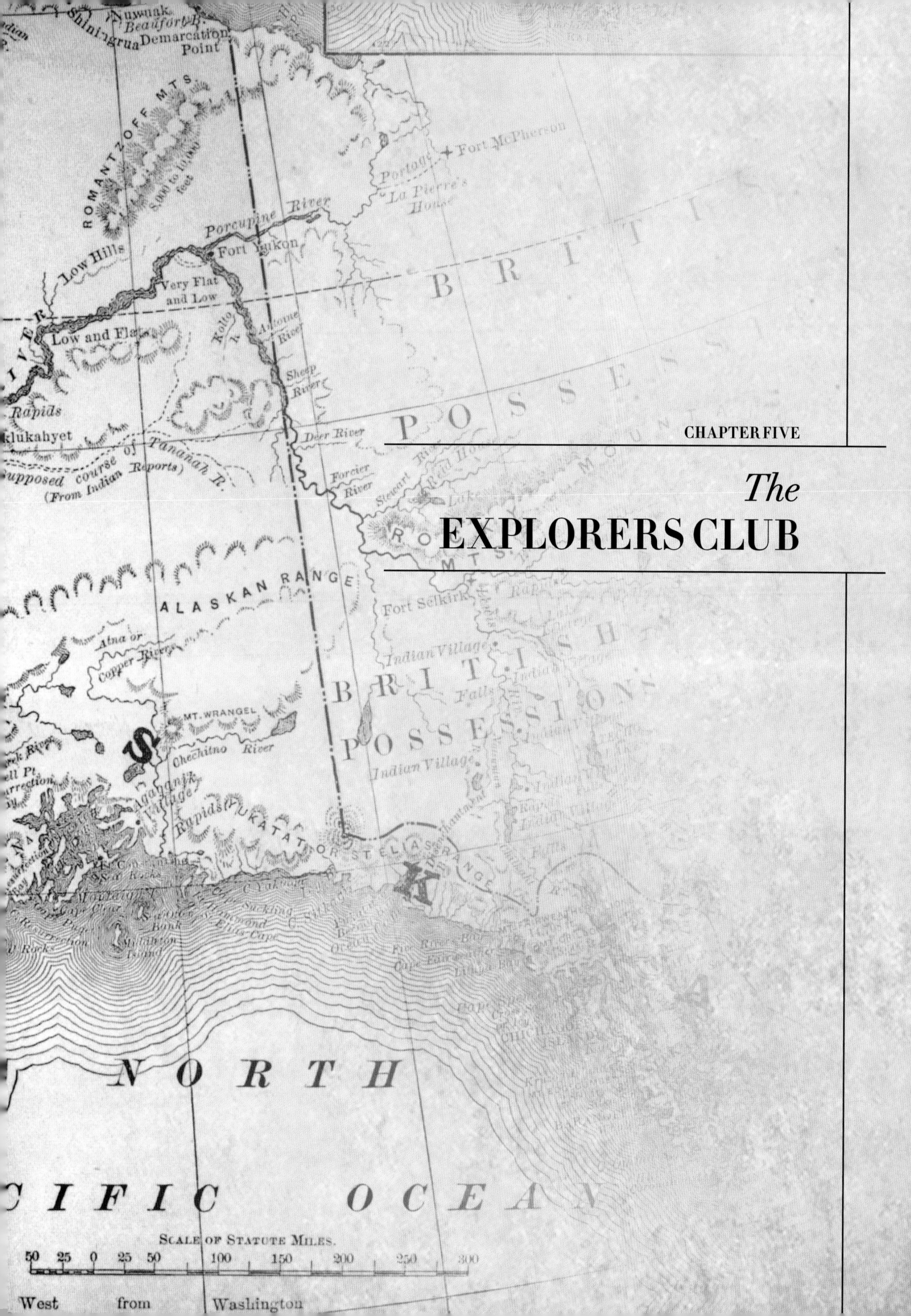

CHAPTER FIVE

The
EXPLORERS CLUB

The Explorers Club

"Last night I was up at the Explorers Club," wrote L. Ron Hubbard from his New York residence on December 13, 1939. "Wilkins and Stefansson and Archbold and ad infinitum were there and they made me much at home." In fact, he was soon to be honored with a full membership (effective February 1940), and thus a long association with those who "had to be big or fall before the unknown." But first let us add a few pertinent details:

Wilkins was, of course, Sir George Hubert Wilkins, the first to fly the Antarctic and second in command of the British Imperial Antarctic Expedition. Stefansson was naturally Vilhjalmur Stefansson of North Canadian and Arctic Circle fame, while Archbold was Richard Archbold of New Guinea exploration. Among other cited qualifications for admission—and requirements for full Explorers Club membership are, indeed, stiff—were the aforementioned LRH additions to West Indies coast pilots from his Caribbean Motion Picture Expedition, the fact he conducted the first complete Puerto Rican mineralogical survey under United States domain and the closure of some thirty hazardous airstrips following from his Department of Commerce report. Finally, let us understand the Explorers Club had been founded in 1904, then stood on 72nd Street (now on 70th Street) in New York City and evoked precisely what one would expect from the realm of grand exploration, including stuffed polar bears on staircase landings, leopard skins across the hearth and a pair of elephant tusks to grace the fireplace. The club also boasted—and still maintains—an astonishing library of field journals and maps from those who actually shaped those maps. Then, too, as Ron's note implies, one could regularly find the likes of Wilkins and Stefansson swapping stories of polar adventure (or periodically seated in the banquet hall to dine on flank steaks cut from a long-frozen mammoth).

More to the point, however, particularly as regards Ron's story, is the famed Explorers Club flag. Awarded to active members in

Left New York address of the world-famed Explorers Club, home to the greatest names in exploration for more than a hundred years

Above
Captain L. Ron Hubbard's Explorers Club bracelet, signifying his membership in that league of adventurous gentlemen

Right
Captain L. Ron Hubbard boldly en route through the Inside Passage while conducting his legendary Alaskan Expedition of 1940

command of or serving with expeditions of legitimate scientific concern, the Explorers Club flag represents an official sanction of exploratory ventures. It has a bold history from Roy Chapman Andrews' descent into the Gobi to Edmund Hillary's ascent of Mount Everest, from the bottom of the ocean to the face of the moon. Moreover, men have suffered beneath it, died beneath it, and those entrusted with it are sincerely implored to "always bear in mind that this flag has been used in the past by many famous persons belonging to the Explorers Club, and that it is a signal honor to carry it."

L. Ron Hubbard first carried the flag aboard a thirty-two-foot ketch on his 1940 Alaskan Radio Experimental Expedition. As the title implies, the voyage called for the testing of a then novel radio navigation device between Puget Sound and the Alaskan Panhandle and, factually, played no insignificant role in the development of the LORAN (*LO*ng *RA*nge *N*avigation) system. Also pertinent to the 1,500-mile voyage was Ron's recharting of an especially treacherous Inside Passage on behalf of the United States Navy Hydrographic Office and his ethnological study of indigenous Aleuts and Haidas. As a further word on the latter, it might be noted LRH was among the first after Franz Boas to examine the mythological heritage of the north coast Indian tribes and was primarily known within exploratory circles as an ethnologist. Not so well known, but nonetheless worth a mention, were the less official ends of the voyage on behalf of the United States Navy. Specifically, Ron was to photograph all coves and channels capable of harboring enemy submarines and thence make his way to the Kuril Islands photographing Japanese warships. Along the way, he not only nabbed an enemy spy, he also braved 180-mile-an-hour winds and commensurate seas off the Aleutians; hence the tattered state of Flag 105—and hence, the irony of what follows here as "It Bears Telling."

Originally appearing in the pages of an Explorers Club anthology entitled, *Through Hell and High Water*, it tells of Ron's "wrestling match" with a Kodiak bear. Inasmuch as the anthology presents only factual accounts of adventures in the field, L. Ron Hubbard's "It Bears Telling" incited no end of discussion. The principal topic being: was it actually possible to survive a hostile encounter with one of North America's most formidable carnivores? Eventually tiring of hearing only about that "damned brownie," Ron furnished his own unvarnished account. It is reprinted as originally published in 1941, replete with an introduction by the editor of *Through Hell and High Water*. ■

The L. Ron Hubbard Series | *Adventurer/Explorer*

A Prefatory Word from the Editor of Through Hell and High Water

I wish Bill Mann was here today. All that expansion at his Zoo in Washington has kept him too closely confined and we don't see enough of him around the Long Table.

There is one question I particularly wanted to ask him. I wanted to know if it was possible for a man to wrestle with a full-grown Kodiak bear and come out on top. I have heard that they are rather unrefined and that most people have been advised to stay away from them. Yet there is a persistent rumor around town that our redheaded Captain Ron Hubbard goes out of his way to pick wrestling matches with Kodiaks. It has even reached the point where ballads are being written about his prowess.

Now, Captain Hubbard left these parts recently on a supposedly scientific expedition. He was even allowed to carry the Club flag, which meant that his purpose was scientific. His schooner *Magician* was well equipped to carry on some badly-needed radio studies and research, but we haven't heard anything about that. Bears are all we hear about.

Have you anything to say for yourself, Ron?

Right The 1941 edition of *Through Hell and High Water,* published by the Explorers Club and presenting "It Bears Telling" by L. Ron Hubbard

IT BEARS TELLING

by L. Ron Hubbard

ENTLEMEN, NOT EVEN HERE am I safe from this continual chatter about bears. I am getting so I can't—oops, I almost made that horrible pun which has been following me about.

To begin, the whole thing is a damned lie. I did not make love to the bear and the bear did not die of longing. Further, I do not make a practice of going around picking on poor, innocent Kodiak bears. The day I arrived in New York City, this thing began: I picked up my phone to hear a cooing voice say, "Cap'n, do you *like* to wrassle with bears?" And since that day I have had no peace. How the story arrived ahead of me I do not know. Personally I tried hard to keep it a dark—I mean the whole thing is a damned lie!

A man can spend endless months of hardship and heroic privation in checking coast pilots; he can squeeze his head to half its width between earphones calculating radio errors; he can brave storm and sudden death in all its most horrible forms in an attempt to increase man's knowledge, and what happens? Is he a hero? Do people look upon his salt-encrusted and exhausted self with awe? Do universities give him degrees and governments commissions? NO! They all look at him with a giggle and ask him if he likes to wrassle with bears. It's an outrage! It's enough to make a man take up paper-doll cutting! Gratitude, bah! Attention and notoriety have centered upon one singular accident—an exaggerated untruth—and the gigantic benefits to the human race are all forgotten!

Gentlemen, examine the facts. A Kodiak bear, known in Alaska as the "brownie," is the world's largest carnivorous animal. He stands as tall as two of us and weighs sixteen hundred active and ferocious pounds. This past autumn in two different parts of Alaska men were attacked by brownies and so badly mauled that one man died and the other will never walk again. And yet you imply that a sane man likes to wrassle with Kodiak bears! Why, compared with a Kodiak, a grizzly is a Teddy bear! No, the whole thing is preposterous and I must ask to be excused.

You say that the rumors still persist and insist that there must be something behind them?

Well—there was such an incident as the one you vaguely mention. But I tell you I had nothing whatever to do with it!

The thing began when a trolling-boat skipper came up alongside a survey—came up alongside a big cutter and asked an officer if he wanted to run up through a passageway generally too shallow and too studded with rocks to admit a larger vessel.

The officer, anticipating nothing, gladly went aboard the small trolling vessel and they shoved off. The boat was about 31 feet long and, because there were only a few pounds of fish in the hold, was somewhat subject to an unstable movement even though the day was calm.

"To begin, the whole thing is a damned lie. I did not make love to the bear and the bear did not die of longing. Further, I do not make a practice of going around picking on poor, innocent Kodiak bears."

The boat chug-chugged between the steep shores of the winding channel and the officer admired the scenery considerably. However, the whole thing was a bit boring, for there is such a thing as too much scenery, even in Alaska.

After some time the attention of the officer was attracted by a bobbing something out in the center of the wide channel. It might be a log or a seal but it was at least something of interest. As the troller approached, the outline of the head began to sharpen. Evidently it was a small black bear, trying stupidly to make headway against a two-knot current and stubbornly refusing to give up the struggle.

The skipper bemoaned the fact that he had no gun aboard and the officer cursed the lack of forethought that had brought him here without a camera.

"Ay vas thinking it vas a shame to lat the bear go," said the skipper.

"Right you are," said the officer. "Isn't there some way we could get him?"

"Maybe if we vent back and got a gun," suggested the skipper.

"It's miles to the ship and he'd be gone by then. I'll tell you, we'll drop a rope over his head and tow him back!"

Nothing seemed simpler and the officer ran off a few fathoms of rope with a running bowline in it and the trolling boat soon overtook the swimming bear. It was easy to slip the noose over the animal's head and make the other fall fast to the ship. This done, the fisherman turned on power and they began to tow the bear along at about four knots.

The bear, however, objected. Water kept getting in his eyes and mouth and the rope around his neck was choking him. Probably he would have gone on having a hard time of it if water in the gas had not made the engine conk.

The fisherman leaped down from wheel to engine and the officer took the helm to guide the boat with what way it had left. No attention was given to the bear for several seconds.

Suddenly the boat reeled under the impact of a terrific blow. The three top gunwale strakes on the starboard side caved in like laths. The boat gave a terrible lurch and several hundred gallons of eager water spewed into the hull.

The officer whirled, to see that their tow was coming aboard! Somehow it had come close to the boat and had clawed up the low side!

The fisherman leaped into the pilothouse from below and the officer leaped for the deck, with some vague idea of shoving the bear back into the water with an oar.

More and more bear had been coming out of the water and the trolling boat was heeling and taking in an ocean at a gulp.

With a mournful wail the fisherman cried, "It vas a *brownie!*"

The officer needed no confirmation. The brute's head, hair plastered down with water—and naturally small anyway—had been wholly deceptive. Streaming and roaring, the brownie got aboard and dived for the officer.

The officer had no wish to match blows with three-quarters of a ton of Kodiak and dodged back around the lump of a pilothouse which stood out of the deck. The bear, making the little boat rock as though a hurricane had hit it, lunged in pursuit. The bear held a grudge because he did not like to be towed at four knots.

"Come in!" screamed the fisherman, meaning the officer, not the bear, and yanked his human passenger into the pilothouse. Together they got the door solidly bolted.

The brownie bent over and glared through the ports of the house; the ports were too small to admit his paws. He buffeted the structure for a while and then, failing to make an impression, gave it up. Besides, he was tired.

He went aft by the fish hatch and sat down, thus bringing the bows out of the water. He panted and clawed at the rope about his neck and cast occasional promises toward the pilothouse.

Below, the fisherman was bailing madly in an attempt to keep the small vessel from swamping but the water was already up to the carburetor and coil of the engine and more came in steadily.

They decided to let the tide carry the boat near some rocks ahead, in the hope that the bear might feel some gratitude for having been ferried there and so go ashore and leave them. Slowly they drifted to the rocks, slid up on one and were held there by the current.

Belatedly it occurred to the men that the bear was still tied to the boat with a nice, strong rope, and if he was to be put ashore something would have to be done about untying him.

The fisherman opened the door a crack. The officer edged slowly toward the cleat and the rope. With a roar and a lunge the bear remembered his revenge. The officer scuttled back, got in, and the bear hit the door.

The movement of the brownie made the boat heel to starboard and water began to pour in with renewed fury. It was certain that if they had the bear another hour they would have to give him the boat.

The tide went slack and then began to run the other way. Evening approached and with it a wind. The officer and the fisherman took turns at the pump and, by strenuously continuing the operation, were able to keep the water from completely drowning the engine. This could not go on forever, they decided.

Finally they had an idea. They took a pike pole which could be reached from the pilothouse port and to the end of it lashed a long, sharp knife. Then, moving slowly so as not to attract the ire of the brownie, began to saw through the line by this remote control.

But when the line was parted the brownie made no effort to avail himself of the fact. He was not grateful. He had calmed considerably and had become interested in the delicious odor of fish which assailed his nostrils. Finally he located the source and with one tap of his paw knocked the top off the fish hold. There he found a number of beautiful fish and proceeded to take one bite from the belly of each, casting the thirty-pound remains overboard.

It was dark now and the tide was falling and soon the trolling boat would be left high on a reef, from which it would probably fall, with no good consequences to itself or anyone aboard.

Desperation caused the two exhausted men to peg chunks of coal at the bear, who had now begun to doze.

The first few blows went unnoticed but finally the bear roused himself, gave the pilothouse a final rush and then, stalking angrily, stepped to the rocks and went ashore.

The men were glad to see him go.

They managed to get the water out of the boat and get the boat off the rocks and the engine going once more. And then they went home.

Now that, gentlemen, is the full and true account of my—of the incident of the bear. It is a lie that anybody broke the bear's heart or that the bear wanted to kiss anybody. It is also a lie that anybody showed the slightest inclination to wrassle that bear. And any songs written about it, and any puns made about it, are libelous. It is enough to be teased about it in Alaska without being teased about it here. In short, the whole thing is a damned lie!

Recipes for Adventure

For all else exploration represents in popular imagination, what is generally unimaginable are the kinds of dishes gracing tables at Explorers Club banquets. Traditionally described as safari dinners, main courses tend to range from the truly exotic to the outright bizarre. In addition to those mammoth steaks exhumed from primeval glaciers, for example, salads were said to have included undigested grass found in the mammoth's belly. Then there was roughriding United States senator Barry Goldwater's "Peggy's Frijoles," American astronaut John Glenn's "muffins" and "ham loaf," followed by locust cakes, lamprey casserole and yellow jacket soup, to name but a few delectable items found in *The Explorers Cookbook: An International Potpourri of Recipes and Tales from World Adventurers*.

The text is more or less self-explanatory. "From men who live the lives of excitement and high adventure most of us only dream about," reads the introductory note, "comes the most non-conforming 'cookbook' ever published...an international potpourri by and about members of the worldwide and world-famed Explorers Club." While by way of a disclaimer, the editors felt obliged to add:

"Many cookbooks are prefaced by statements claiming laboratory testing, home-kitchen testing, standard measurements and all that sort of thing. Not *this* 'cookbook'!

"Of course, we did find a good many of the recipes so tantalizing we could hardly wait to prepare them for 'home tasting.' But because explorers under survival conditions are known to eat virtually anything, some of these recipes we recommend only to the adventuresome spirit, strong of heart and stronger of stomach, who can do his own testing and tasting."

Ron's own recipes are from a similarly exotic corner of the menu and the Explorers Club advice holds true: this is the real stuff, and only for those with adventurous spirits and stomachs to match. From his various Caribbean voyages comes "Iguana à Rotisserie" on a broad leaf. From his upcoming North African/Mediterranean expedition comes his charred sheep's head (replete with eyes) and his small white snails with licorice. Also included here is Ron's own introductory *bon appétit*.

Boubbouche

In French restaurants all over the world, one can order the fat gray Burgundy snails.

But the "boubbouche" as they call them in the beautiful old city of Fez, served hot or cold in delightful pottery bowls with slithers of wild acacia to eat them with, are small and white.

The Arabs cook them in a highly perfumed sauce—which they say, purifies the blood, gives one appetite and ensures no upset of the stomach in the rich dishes to follow. In fact, the bouillon is often served, on its own, as an aperitif.

First of all, you have to keep the escargots cool and dry in a perforated dish, "fasting" for several days.

They are washed no less than seven times: 3 times in fresh water, once in heavy brine, and 3 times again in fresh water, before straining.

A pot of water is put to boil, with just enough water to cover the snails. As soon as it boils, put in

> a large pinch of squalls of anises
> a large pinch of caraway
> two or three pieces of licorice
> a soup spoon of thyme
> a small handful of green tea
> a twig of sage
> a twig of absinthe
> a small bunch of mint
> a twig of marjoram
> the peel of one bitter orange
> a pinch of pimento from the Sudan
> salt to taste.

Stir it a little, add the escargots, cover and let cook for at least two hours.

Put the whole into a bowl to cool. Just before serving, it may be reheated.

A heady dish!

Recipes for Adventure   111

Bou i laff

A variation on the well-known shish kebab or shashlik can be found further west where Araby stretches past the blue Med to the grayer Atlantic.

It bears the name of BOU I LAFF; it is quickly prepared and takes no time at all to cook—a great advantage to a hungry wanderer after a long day in the lower Atlas.

About 1 pound of calf's liver is fried very quickly on all sides then cut into cubes of about an inch. The cubes are dusted with salt, a touch of cumin and just a "soupçon" of red pepper. Then, wrapped in strips of sheep's caul, they are put on skewers and lightly grilled.

Not a dish for the formal feast in the richly rugged tent, but first-class while waiting for the choua, which has been cooking for some time, awaiting your return.

Choua

They put a large fat piece of lamb—shoulder and cutlets at least—rubbed in salt and ground saffron, wrapped in a serviette into the top of a double boiler covered and bound together with cord. It's left over a strong fire for about 3 hours.

It needs no further seasoning except maybe for some salt and ground cumin.

The *head* of the sheep is often cooked this way. The head is shaved and the remaining hairs are charred.

The horns are snapped off with a quick blow of the chopper. The head is shook briskly to get the worms out of mouth and ears.

Another blow of the chopper parts the head in two so the brain can be removed, washed in ashes, swilled and cooked separately.

The head is wrapped in the napkin, and is steamed.

The eye is the tasty bit. You gently nudge it out with a finger, extract and throw away the iris, season with a little cumin and salt. And be very sure to enjoy it hugely.

In some parts of the Atlas, the Arabs have round ovens made of lime and earth. The ovens produce a strange but delicious breakfast.

At the break of day, out from the ovens comes a procession of lightly grilled, braised heads.

Cleaned with salt water, sheared and charred, brains removed, they are put in the warm oven on layers of grass as the sun goes down.

The openings of the ovens are stopped up with mud and grass.

Opened in the morning, the most delicious aroma preludes a novel and unforgettable breakfast.

So delicate is the flavor of cheek and tongue that only a touch of salt and ground cumin is needed.

Iguana à Rotisserie

Sitting with a chief in the back swamps of Central America I was served some delicious white meat on a broad leaf.

Suddenly I was struck by the fact I had seen no chickens in that area. Alert, I asked politely what it was.

"Lizard's tail," I was told.

When I had very politely finished dinner, the chief was so pleased at my obvious enjoyment (an explorer has to be a consummate actor at times), that he showed me how it was prepared.

The iguana comes in various sizes. Alike they are shot with arrows despite their swiftness.

Only the tail is used. It is up to a third the reptile's length.

This tail is cut off close to the body. A stick is forced into it to keep it straight and it is toasted, while being rotated over hot coals.

The tail is then skinned and laid on any broad green leaf.

The meat, aside from a slight greenish cast, is not really detectable from the breast of chicken.

I am told that there are various different ways of catching and cooking iguanas that vary from area to area.

However, the point I wish to make is that when eating with polite formal chiefs it is wisest not to ask, halfway through a meal, what one is eating.

Greco-Roman ruins of Sardinia, where Mission into Time exploration laid bare many a forgotten footnote of history

CHAPTER SIX

Mission into
TIME

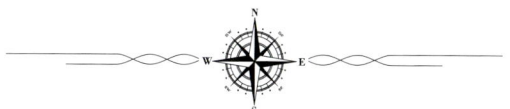

Mission into Time

"Probably the strangest place an explorer can go," L. Ron Hubbard declared as of late 1949, "is inside." He was, of course, alluding to the human mind, or what he otherwise described as that *Terra Incognita* "half an inch back of our foreheads." What is not generally realized, however, and what inevitably leads us to Ron's final expedition, is the fact that his first formal explanation of this *Terra Incognita,* and thus the advent of Dianetics, most appropriately appeared in *The Explorers Journal*.

His reasoning was simple enough: "The earth's frontiers are being rapidly gobbled up by the fleet flight of planes. The stars are not yet reached. But there still exists a dark unknown which, if a strange horizon for an adventurer, is nevertheless capable of producing some adventures scarcely rivaled by Livingstone." Then, too, as he pointed out, the principles of Dianetics were just as applicable to the far-flung explorer as the man on the street and, in fact, many an expedition was known to have failed for want of clear thinking in moments of crises. Thus, and specifically in the name of grand exploration, members and associates of the Explorers Club were actually the first to examine L. Ron Hubbard's official description of Dianetics.

All essential theory was provided: how human memory is retained and retrieved, how physical pain and unconsciousness suffered through the course of expeditionary work may affect behavior and health, and how the techniques of Dianetics may be used to alleviate such travail. Also included was Dianetics theory pertaining to the selection of expeditionary personnel and a synopsis of Dianetics procedures for use in the field.

With the founding of Scientology three years later and what may be described as the first scientific explanation of spiritual matters, Ron's point of comparison grew even sharper:

"As a member of that crew of experts on the subject, the Explorers Club, as one who has

Left Aboard the *Enchanter* prior to launch of Mission into Time, 1968

Right
Roman ruins at Nora in Sardinia. On the off chance archeologists had failed to discover a secret entrance to the Temple of Tanit, LRH provided scouting teams with an explicit description of dimensions: six feet deep, fourteen feet in length and a distinctive pattern of tiles at the mouth of the passage. And, to be sure, on chipping away 2,500 years of encrusted soil, there lay a secret passage at the base of the Tanit Tower—*exactly as described*.

plowed keel into seven seas, who has ducked shots fired in anger and watched others fail to duck, I can verify that when all horizons are measured, all swamps mapped, all deserts charted and supplied with water and instant rescue, there will yet be a world of unknown frights and glooms and cheers to explore. There will yet be a universe of adventure left, a universe sufficiently powerful to daunt the last few thousand years of thinking men—You. The universe of You."

To which we might add that when speaking of "the universe of You," he was referencing an altogether magnificent view of our capabilities as immortal and infinite spiritual beings.

If such a statement seems at odds with generally accepted expeditionary matters, it is not necessarily so and, in fact, more than a few Explorers Club fellows tell of witnessing wonders that forever left them questioning what is scientifically acceptable. (Subsequent to his 1971 lunar expedition, *Apollo 14* astronaut Edgar Mitchell, for example, dedicated himself to what is best described as paranormal research.) Then, too, and even more pertinent, is all that falls under para-archaeological research, including the truly astonishing discoveries of those who would seem to have "remembered" key archaeological sites from former lifetimes.

The particulars vary, but accepting a central revelation of Scientology wherein Man is held to possess experience from many lives across many centuries, then logically that experience should have some relevance to archaeological discovery. Among other frequently cited cases are those of Tibetan and Indian children who reportedly recall not only former incarnations, but the verifiable location of buried relics in places they had never visited. Then again, there are the various cases of Scientologists recalling an otherwise forgotten name from a former lifetime only to find that same name on an equally forgotten gravestone. Finally, and if only for the sake of argument, one cannot ignore Heinrich Schliemann's suggestions of something similar at work when, essentially armed with but a copy of the *Iliad* and a lifelong obsession, he unearthed the ruins of Troy.

If altogether more scientific in design, Ron's proposal was ultimately just as adventurous. Was it possible, he asked, to verify the details of past-life memories with the material record from archaeological investigation? As a preliminary word, he would have us understand that by past-life memories he was specifically referring to the "whole track" and defined it as the "moment-to-moment record of a person's existence in this universe

Above
The *Avon River* (LEFT) served as the expedition's base, while *Enchanter* (RIGHT) acted as scout vessel

Right
The expeditionary vessel, *Enchanter*

in picture and impression form." As for the particulars—how individual impressions are recorded, stored and recalled—this is the stuff of Dianetics. Yet suffice it to say, those impressions are real, and verifiably so. Thus the question became not whether whole track memory was valid, but could one tap it for archaeological advancement? As another preliminary word, readers should understand that similar experimentation through the 1970s and 1980s, including Explorers Club fellow Stephan A. Schwartz's "psychic" search for the tomb of Alexander the Great, were essentially derivative and Ron was categorically the first to explore this dimension.

Initial correspondence only peripherally references the matter. "We are organizing the Ocean Archaeological Expedition," he informed New York and London curators in May of 1961 and described a forthcoming hunt for artifacts "pertaining to Mediterranean culture likely to be found in cities and harbors of past ages or cargoes carried in ancient vessels." Although then receiving Explorers Club flag number 163, and proceeding with the refit of a Fairmile Class "B" Motor Launch, it was not until September of 1967 that plans came to real fruition—by which point, the Ocean Archaeological Expedition had become a broader Hubbard Geological Survey Expedition and the Fairmile replaced with two vessels, the double-ended, high-sided ketch *Enchanter* and a 150-foot North Sea trawler known as the *Avon River*. Stated aims were likewise grander: "To complete a general geological survey of a belt from Italy, through Greece and the Red Sea and Egypt and along the Gulf of Aden and the East Coast of Africa," and simultaneously "to find and examine relics and artifacts and so possibly amplify man's knowledge of history." While if he yet made no official mention of how such relics and artifacts might be found, preliminary exercises told all.

Primarily along the coast of southern England, teams were dispatched on foot or aboard small crafts with LRH-sketched maps of minor archaeological sites drawn from whole track memory. That is, without aid of local historical guides or previous investigation, Hubbard Geological Survey teams were directed to long-submerged or buried ruins on and around England's southern and western coasts. In the main, sites were Anglo-Saxon or Roman and insignificant. But having determined the location of those sites solely from whole track memory—which is to say, having recalled specific features of a two-thousand-year-old landscape—Ron was able to successfully direct

Above
Route of the Mission into Time expedition

his teams to otherwise forgotten ruins. Of course, the ramifications are enormous—scientifically, religiously and philosophically enormous. Yet setting aside the greater significance of what whole track memory implies, let us continue south to Las Palmas in the Canary Islands, where his vessels were to receive a final fitting, and thence on to the Spanish port of Valencia for the formal commencement of Ron's "A Test of Whole Track Recall," or what is best remembered as his Mission into Time.

With the *Avon River* as Ron's primary expeditionary vessel and *Enchanter* as scout, survey parties would finally touch upon several Mediterranean ports. In the main, however, sights primarily focused upon Sardinia, Sicily and the coast of Tunisia. Historically, of course, these are among the world's richest waters, with continual traffic for at least some five thousand years; while Sicily, in particular, had been much disputed and repeatedly built upon. Of particular interest, however, were later Greek, Carthaginian and Roman-Phoenician remains from approximately 200 B.C. to A.D. 300. Moreover, what with infamously restrictive excavation ordinances along virtually all European and North African shores, attention lay not so much on the recovery of artifacts as the location of neglected remains.

The mood is fairly prosaic through accounts of what followed. Emphasis lay on logistics, on the physical safety of an inexperienced crew, on the management of vessels and the refinement of rules by which missions were best conducted. Indeed, it was specifically from this Mission into Time that a good many of Ron's now famous mission policies were derived, including the use of clay models to represent prospective sites. As further word on those clay representations, readers should understand the device was both unique and, frankly, ingenious. For in addition to providing survey parties with a lay of the land before actually setting out, the models served as a tangible verification of the sites. That is, did the LRH clay model—sculpted, we must remember, without aid of maps or visuals—in fact correspond to what survey parties found? As an ancillary word, it might also be noted that survey parties would tell of repeatedly returning to the *Avon River* for a second and third study of those clay models or until, at

122   THE L. RON HUBBARD SERIES | *Adventurer/Explorer*

Left
The long-concealed entrance below the ruins of Tanit—untouched since before the birth of Christ and unearthed solely through L. Ron Hubbard's recollection of an earlier civilization

Below
LRH notes on Sardinian digs from Mission into Time

last, the actual landscape began to assume a recognizable form.

Meanwhile, in a typically workaday fashion, Ron would continue to tell of "writing up an area, never having been into it in this lifetime, saying exactly what the score was with regard to that area and then sending out parties to see if they could exactly locate and estimate whether or not these recalls were exactly correct." While as yet another note on logistics, it might be added that those survey teams would generally launch in small sail craft from the *Avon River* or set out with the *Enchanter*—which, in turn, required a skill of seamanship in short supply, and thus Ron's continual attention to nautical matters to ensure all parties, as he quipped, "carry on our happy, nautical way and return back from where we came all in one piece." Yet even the most perfunctory description of proceedings does not fail to evoke something wondrous.

For example, in the first days of February 1968, the expedition approached a first "target" lying on the southeast tip of Sardinia, where Ron had sketched a second century B.C. foundation described as the Temple of Tanit and originally dedicated to the Carthage patroness of the same

Mission into Time   123

Above
An expeditionary dig on Sicily where LRH recalled a domed Roman tomb near Cape Orlando and where subsequent excavation indeed revealed a long-buried sepulcher from the trailing days of the Roman Empire

Right
The tower near Castellammare, Sicily. An LRH description of the ruin, exclusively based on "whole track" recall, read: "Just outside the entrance and eighteen inches through the wall as you face the tower it will be hollow." Also noted were concave walls and blue tiles—all of which were found intact and *precisely* as Ron indicated.

name (or alleged variant of the Phoenician Asherat, mother of the sea). Although the structure itself had been known since 1952, what Ron recalled as a lower, concealed entrance was not. In other words—and this again without ever laying eyes upon the structure—LRH sketches indicated the presence of an unexcavated entrance *below* the temple base. Whereupon, as he so perfunctorily explains: "Missions were sent ashore to survey and map the area to see if they couldn't discover this old secret entrance to the temple as the target that would demonstrate the whole track memory.

"We lowered boats and rowed back and forth and sent people ashore. They looked it all over and finally came up with a result."

That is, as one of the actual survey party proceeded to explain, having determined a "ditch" at the base of the temple, "we scraped around at the bottom of the ditch and found it was tiled underneath a thin layer of dust and dirt...until we were quite convinced that this was the ditch that led into the basement of the temple. So, that was totally proven and accurate."

Similarly, LRH sketches of a domed Roman tomb in the center of a graveyard on the island of Sicily, five miles from a castle near Cape Orlando, proved just as accurate and were all the more impressive for the fact that indicated gravestones had long been dismantled for the construction of stables and so appeared on no local maps. In any case, as yet another of the survey party explained: "We traveled for about a day and a half or two and there was the beach just as was mapped out. Ron had also given us, before our arrival, a second map that showed exactly the plan of the tower, how it would look, how the cellar would look and the whole construction of the tower. We went up to the tower and dug around for several hours and found exactly the structure that was indicated."

Then followed equally true LRH sketches of Roman-Carthaginian ruins in Tunisia, also long buried beneath modern structures and likewise disregarded on local guides, followed by his indication of only-just-discovered Phoenician-Carthage ruins beneath the harbor waters. Finally, and in genuinely startling detail, he was able to describe the view from a vessel's bow at the mouth of a never previously visited Tunisian cove, right down to the boulder formations. That is, before sailing from the port of Tunis, Ron had sketched an otherwise insignificant stretch of coast to the south. Arriving in utter darkness, he confidently informed the *Avon River* crew, "Your ship's bow (it was very dark) is now pointing at a pointed hill on the east-facing side of the cove and there's

124   THE L. RON HUBBARD SERIES | *Adventurer/Explorer*

Right
View from the bay of a forlorn Sicilian ruin: "And it was rather interesting to see the barrenness and desertedness of these ancient cities"—LRH

Below inset
Enchanter crew preparing for departure to another target

a boulder there…" Whereupon, survey teams waited until first light and observed precisely the same.

Peripheral LRH comments are likewise fascinating. In the first place, he explained, whole track research (when combined with the material record) suggested ancient populations to have been far greater than typically reckoned—at least five times the generally acknowledged figure and thus explaining, for example, the 160 cities once gracing a now relatively barren Sicily. Also habitually underestimated were troop strengths of the ancient world, since archaeological figures regularly neglected to factor in the five-to-one logistical backbone of armies. Thus, the pointed LRH remark, "The archaeologist makes a fundamental and fantastic error. When he counts the number of soldiers engaged in a battle, he of course omits the numbers of supply sergeants, clerks and, of course, 'super generals' who were sitting back of the lines." Then, too, and herein lay an overall LRH conclusion reflected in later essays on equitable administration for which he is equally famous: the ancient world did not ultimately succumb to a barbarian onslaught; it had succumbed to internal strife and its own political mismanagement.

Above
Metal detectors were employed to help locate long-buried ruins

Right
Roman ruins near Carthage in modern Tunisia. Here, too, LRH recall proved stunningly accurate, right down to rock formations above long-forgotten coves.

What else might be concluded from those extraordinary five weeks is, of course, a vast subject, and bears upon virtually every popular conception of the ancient world. It also, of course, bears heavily upon the ways in which we might learn about that world, and, in fact, Mission into Time inevitably inspired several similar projects, including famed "psychic" experimentation at the Stanford Research Institute under United States Navy subsidy. Also, as suggested, the parallels to fellow Explorers Club member Stephan A. Schwartz's Alexandria Project are far too striking to be ignored. Yet declaring the ultimate realm of adventure to lie within the human spirit, within a universe of the mind which "minute by minute opens and unfolds," Ron himself put such matters aside and returned to his primary track of exploration, the development of Scientology. Not that he would cease plowing keel into foreign seas or measuring distant horizons. But when speaking of exploration, he thereafter spoke of nothing less than discovering "the infinity of infinities." ∎

Epilogue

"Adventure is my guidon," declared L. Ron Hubbard long ago and proceeded to etch that phrase across many a dim land, distant sea and limitless sky. He further etched it across that dimmest realm of all, that *Terra Incognita* within us, and so came to embody all we imagine when hearing the words "Men had to be big or fall before the unknown."

But lest we miss the greater lesson from these pages, let us close with what Ron himself would have us bear in mind. Yes, there is much to be said for the lure of strange horizons and faraway lands, but let us also not forget, "Adventure, I well know, is in the heart, not in the view."

APPENDIX

Glossary | 135
Index | 175

GLOSSARY

abbreviated: reduced in length. Page 43.

absinthe: an herb having a bitter, slightly aromatic, taste. Page 111.

acacia: a small tree, growing in warm climates, that has small fluffy yellow flowers and narrow leaves. Page 111.

advent: an important arrival, especially one that marks the beginning of a new era in the history of a people. Page 38.

Adventure: an American pulp magazine founded in 1910. One of the pulps produced by Popular Publications, the magazine featured adventure and fiction stories. Page 2.

aerial knight: an air force pilot who engages other pilots, often in single combat, like a knight of the Middle Ages. Page 69.

aft: toward the rear of a ship. Page 107.

air meet: a gathering of people taking part in or viewing aerial sporting activities. The word *meet* means a sports gathering of competitive events. Air meets involve activities such as air racing and *stunt flying,* skillful changes of position of an aircraft, such as flying upside down or in a circle. Competitors are judged on style, accuracy, speed, altitude, etc. Air meets have been popular since the early 1900s, when the airplane was invented. Page 54.

airstrip: a small landing field having only one runway. Page 69.

Alaskan expedition: the *Alaskan Radio Experimental Expedition,* a 1,500-mile (2,400-kilometer) voyage conducted to provide data for correct mapping of the coastline between the northwestern shores of the continental US and the southern part of Alaska. The expedition resulted in photographs and navigational information to correct the previously mischarted coastline. Page 10.

Aleutians: a chain of islands off southwest Alaska that separates the Bering Sea in the north from the Pacific Ocean in the south. Page 100.

Aleuts: Native North American people of the Aleutian Islands and the western Alaska Peninsula. *See also* **Aleutians.** Page 100.

Alexander the Great: (356–323 B.C.) military general and king of Macedonia (an ancient kingdom in northern Greece) who conquered much of what was then considered the civilized world, stretching from present-day Greece to India. His tomb was the most renowned and respected shrine in the Roman Empire and stood for centuries at the heart of the greatest Greek city in the world, Alexandria. At the end of the fourth century A.D., it disappeared without a trace and has been one of the most searched-for tombs of all. Page 120.

Alexandria Project: a project that attempted to locate historical structures of Alexandria, Egypt, conducted in the late 1970s by psychic archaeologist Stephan A. Schwartz. The city of Alexandria, which lies on the Mediterranean, is the principal port of Egypt and the second-largest city in the country. Founded as the capital of Egypt in 331 B.C. by Alexander the Great, the city grew to become one of the largest, most impressive cities of the ancient world. Due to sinking of the land, earthquakes and other natural disasters, much of the ancient city lies under water in the harbor, leading to many attempts to locate and recover the ancient buildings, statues and artifacts. Page 128.

alluvial: found in *alluvium,* a deposit of soil formed in river valleys from material washed down by the river. Page 28.

altimeter: an instrument for showing height above sea level, used especially in an aircraft. Page 53.

Americano: Spanish for a person from North America, used here in reference to the United States. Page 29.

amiable: friendly in nature, not aggressive; not threatening harm. Page 36.

ancillary: supplying something additional, such as data or information. Page 122.

Andersonville: a town in southeastern Indiana, a state in the north central United States. Page 79.

Andrews, Roy Chapman: (1884–1960) US author and explorer. Between 1916 and 1930 Andrews led expeditions in parts of Asia. In the Gobi Desert he discovered remains of types of dinosaurs not previously known and the first dinosaur eggs ever found. *See also* **Gobi.** Page 100.

anent: in regard to; about; concerning. Page 95.

Anglo-Saxon: of or relating to the *Anglo-Saxons,* the Germanic people that settled in Britain beginning in the fifth century A.D. Page 120.

annals: historical records generally. Page 10.

anthology: a book or other collection of selected writings by various authors, usually in the same literary form or the same period or on the same subject. Page 100.

Antilles: a chain of islands in the West Indies, divided into two parts, the one including Cuba, Hispaniola, Jamaica and Puerto Rico (Greater Antilles), the other including a large arc of smaller islands to the southeast and south (Lesser Antilles). *See also* **Lesser Antilles.** Page 20.

aperitif: something, such as a drink, taken before a meal to stimulate the appetite. Page 111.

Araby: *Arabia,* in reference to regions of southwestern Asia and northern Africa where Arabic is spoken. Page 112.

Archbold: Richard Archbold (1907–1976), American explorer. During the 1930s, Archbold financed and conducted explorations in New Guinea. It was during one of his 1938 expedition flights that a large population of Stone Age-level people was spotted, living in a remote mountain valley. Until this time, these people, the Dani, had been completely isolated from any contact with the outside world. Page 99.

Argosy: an American fiction magazine published by the Frank A. Munsey Company, first produced in the late 1800s. Containing science fiction, fantasy and other genres, *Argosy* featured some of the best adventure writers of the twentieth century. (The word *argosy* originally meant a large merchant ship and figuratively came to mean a rich, plentiful store or supply of something.) Page 49.

Army Air Corps: an air combat corps under the control of the United States Army from 1926 to 1941. After various reorganizations, this corps became the US Air Force in 1947. Page 84.

Arrow Sport: a small biplane (having two sets of wings, one above the other) built during the 1920s and 1930s by the Arrow Aircraft and Motor Company of Nebraska. The Arrow Sport featured side-by-side seating in an open cockpit equipped with dual controls. It had a maximum speed of 105 miles per hour (169 kilometers per hour) and a range of 280 miles (450 kilometers). Page 69.

Asherat: prominent Middle Eastern goddess, viewed as the mother of the gods and of the sea, hence also as the guardian of sailors. Page 124.

assay: the analysis of a substance by weighing, measuring, calculating, etc., so as to determine the proportions of something valuable, such as a metal contained in an ore. Page 47.

astride: on top of and with a leg on each side (of something, such as a horse). Page 2.

Atlas: a large range of mountains extending 1,500 miles (2,400 kilometers) through three countries of northwestern Africa (Morocco, Algeria and Tunisia). Page 112.

Au: (as noted on hand-drawn map) the symbol for the element gold. From the Latin word *aurum,* gold. Page 32.

audacious: bold and daring; adventurous. Page 19.

avows: declares as a fact. Page 75.

B

back debt: literally, a debt that is still owed, used figuratively to mean a feeling of obligation or gratitude for a favor that one feels must still be returned. Page 60.

badlands: an extensive area of heavily eroded, uncultivatable land with little vegetation. Page 2.

balloon sleeves: short sleeves with a rounded appearance, similar to that of a balloon. Page 43.

Baltimore: a city of northern Maryland, an eastern state of the United States. It has been a busy seaport since the eighteenth century. Page 17.

barnstorming: in the early days of aviation, touring (the country) giving short airplane rides, exhibitions of stunt flying, etc. This term comes from the use of barns as hangars. Page 64.

barracuda: a large fierce fish with sharp teeth that lives in warm seas. Page 21.

Barrio del Carmen: a district (barrio) of the city of Guayama, in southeastern Puerto Rico. Page 44.

BBs: small round metal balls, whose size (.18 inch or .46 centimeter in diameter) is designated as *BB*. Used for firing from guns (called *BB guns*) that operate by air pressure. Page 61.

beachcombing: (said of a person) loafing on beaches, living on what one can beg or find and sell. Page 29.

Beallsville: a town in central Maryland, a state in the eastern United States, on the Atlantic coast. Page 47.

beanbag: a small cloth bag filled with dried beans or something similar, thrown or otherwise used in children's games. Page 33.

beckoning: extending interest or attraction (to someone or something); tempting. Page 70.

begrudge: be unwilling to give or pay something. Page 29.

bemoaned: expressed regret over something. Page 106.

bends: a condition marked by joint pain, nausea, loss of motion and breathing difficulties experienced by divers who emerge too quickly from a pressurized environment such as deep water. It is caused by the formation of nitrogen bubbles in the blood and tissues. Page 49.

Bermuda: a group of islands in the North Atlantic, 580 miles (935 kilometers) east of North Carolina. Bermuda is a self-governing colony of the United Kingdom and a popular resort. Page 17.

biplane: an airplane with two sets of wings, one above the other. Page 54.

bite, at a: in sections, each one viewed figuratively as portions of a whole. Page 60.

Blackfoot: any of the group of Native North American peoples including the Blackfeet of Montana and several tribes now living in Canada. This group controlled areas that were fought over by fur traders in the 1800s. Page 2.

black sand: a dark-colored sand having a high concentration of heavy minerals such as iron. Black sand can also contain gold, since gold is also heavy, but separating the tiny particles of gold from the black sand is a time-consuming process. Page 36.

blood and thunder: bloodshed, violence and uproar similar to what is found in adventure stories. Page 45.

blood brother: either one of two men or boys who have sworn mutual loyalty and friendship, typically by a ceremony involving a superficial cut in the skin and the mingling (mixing) of each other's blood. Page 2.

Boas, Franz: (1858–1942) German-born American anthropologist who stressed the importance of field research (studying a people by living among them) in studying human cultures. Many of his theories were based on his research among the Native North American peoples of the Pacific Northwest. Page 100.

bodice: a type of close-fitting vest. Page 43.

boisterous: 1. full of lively enthusiasm and energy. Page 7.
2. characterized by noisy, cheerful activity. Page 36.

bonanza: an extremely valuable mineral deposit; a source that yields great riches, as a very rich vein or pocket of ore. Page 29.

bowline, running: a type of knot that forms a noose with the knot below the opening of the loop. The noose can then be thrown over something that is out of reach. Page 106.

bow(s): a nautical term for the exterior of the forward end of a ship. Page 107.

box kite: literally, a kite without a tail, consisting of two open-ended boxes joined by thin sticks. Used here figuratively to refer to a glider. Page 60.

braised: cooked slowly in a little fat and liquid in a tightly closed container (properly with a charcoal fire above and below). Page 112.

British Columbian: of or having to do with British Columbia, a province in western Canada on the Pacific coast. Page 10.

British Secret Service: the branch of the British Government that conducts secret investigations, especially investigations into the military strength of other nations. Page 8.

Briton: someone who was born or raised in Great Britain or who is a citizen of Great Britain. Page 35.

broncs, breaking range: taming wild or partly tamed horses of the range (large area of open land, as in the western United States) to a point where they can be saddled and ridden without trying to throw off riders. Page 2.

brownie: a Kodiak bear, also called *big brown bear,* whose coat is yellowish to dark brown in color. *See also* **Kodiak bear.** Page 100.

brush with (something): a brief encounter, especially an occasion when one nearly experiences something unpleasant. Page 54.

buccaneer(s): any of the pirates who raided Spanish colonies and ships along the American coast in the second half of the seventeenth century. Page 25.

bucko: young man; fellow. Page 25.

bullion: gold in the form of bars. Page 29.

bumper: a horizontal bar across the front or back of a motor vehicle to reduce damage in a collision. *Towed from a bumper* means that the glider was pulled by means of a rope tied to the rear bumper of a car until, with enough speed, it could rise and begin flying. Page 53.

burned road: drove very fast. Page 77.

Butte: a city in southwest Montana, a mining center. Page 43.

byroads, on the: living in areas of the country that are not on the main roads but are on the side roads, those that carry a small volume of traffic. Page 82.

caballero: a cowboy or horseman, based on the Spanish word *caballo,* horse. Page 37.

cabaret: a restaurant or nightclub providing short programs of live entertainment. Page 43.

cable tool drilling: also called *percussion drilling,* a method of oil drilling using a drill bit that is repeatedly lifted and dropped by a hoisting cable. The force of the impact crushes the material at the bottom of the well. Page 94.

calculus: a form of mathematics used to make calculations dealing with things in a state of change. In calculus, irregular shapes can be measured or the rate of speed of an accelerating rocket can be determined. Page 10.

called, have (one's) hand: have (one's) statements questioned to find out the source of (one's) information. From the game of poker, in reference to a call for each player to lay down his hand (the cards he is holding) face up so everyone can see who is holding which cards and the winner can be determined. Page 94.

camaraderie: a feeling of close friendship and trust among a particular group of people. Page 1.

Canadian border, lost: a reference to a 1931 United States Geological Survey team of which L. Ron Hubbard was a member. The team was to locate damaged or destroyed US/Canada border markers in the northeastern state of Maine to settle the geographic limit of the United States. Page 10.

Canary Islands: a group of Spanish islands in the Atlantic Ocean located southwest of Spain and about 60 miles (97 kilometers) off the northwest coast of the mainland of Africa. Page 122.

Canton: city in southern China and chief port of the region; a former name of Guangzhou. Page 35.

Cantonese: of Canton (a city in southern China) or its people, language or culture. Page 9.

Cape Orlando: a point on the northern coast of Sicily, near the eastern end of the island. Page 122.

Capitol Hill: literally, the hill in Washington, DC, which is the location of the *Capitol,* the building where the United States Congress meets. *Congress* is the lawmaking body of the US Government and the term *Capitol Hill* is also used figuratively to refer to the lawmaking body itself. Page 84.

Cap'n: *captain,* used as a title or term of address. Page 105.

Captain Courageous: a designation given in praise of a leader of a group or team and used here ironically. Page 20.

caraway: a type of herb cultivated for its fragrant seeds, which are used as a flavoring in various foods. Page 111.

carburetor: a device in an internal-combustion engine that mixes liquid fuel and air in the correct proportions, vaporizes them (makes them into a fine mist) and transfers the mixture into the engine, where it is exploded to provide power. Page 107.

Carib: a member of a group of Indian peoples previously dominant in the Lesser Antilles, now found in small numbers in a few areas of the West Indies and in parts of Central America and northeastern South America. Page 38.

carnivore: an animal that eats other animals; a flesh-eating animal. Page 100.

Carthaginian: of *Carthage,* a powerful ancient city of the northern coast of Africa near present-day Tunis, capital of Tunisia. The city was founded in the ninth century B.C. In 146 B.C., following a series of wars with Rome, Carthage was destroyed and its territory was taken over by the Romans. Page 122.

Cascades: also *Cascade Range,* a chain of mountains in northwestern United States and southwestern Canada that lies about 100 to 150 miles (160 to 240 kilometers) inland from the Pacific coast. The name of the range refers to the numerous small, steep waterfalls (cascades) found in a section of the chain. The highest mountain in the Cascades is Mount Rainier, 14,410 feet (4,392 meters), located in west central Washington State. Page 4.

cast: 1. direct (something, such as a look, glance or the like). Page 107.
2. cause to move by throwing. Page 108.
3. a modification of the appearance of a substance by a trace of some added color. Page 113.

Castellammare: a city on the northwest coast of the island of Sicily, in full, Castellammare del Golfo. It is located on the Gulf of Castellammare, approximately 50 miles (80 kilometers) from Palermo, Sicily's largest city. Page 122.

Castile: also *Castilian,* the variety of Spanish spoken in Castile, now the standard form of the language in Spain. Castile is a region and former kingdom in north and central Spain. Page 32.

catcher's mitt: in the game of baseball, a rounded glove with one section for the four fingers and another for the thumb and having the palm of the hand protected by a thick padding. It is used by the *catcher*, the player stationed behind the batter who catches pitched balls that have not been hit by the batter. Page 62.

catwalk: a very narrow metal walkway on some small planes that runs from the cockpit to the engine, for performing any needed engine maintenance while airborne, especially on very long flights. Page 73.

caul: the fatty membrane surrounding the intestines. Page 112.

chandler: also *ship chandler,* a dealer in supplies and equipment for ships and boats. Page 19.

chaw: a piece of something (usually of tobacco), suitable to be held in the mouth and chewed. Page 25.

Chesapeake Bay: a long, narrow arm of the Atlantic Ocean that runs north from the coast of the state of Virginia and divides the state of Maryland into two parts. It is 200 miles (320 kilometers) long and from 4 to 40 miles (6 to 64 kilometers) wide. Page 14.

chopper: a cutting tool with a handle and a sharp broad blade, used especially for chopping an animal's body. Page 112.

choua: a Moroccan meat dish made with lamb, cooked by steaming. Page 112.

cine: a film theater. Page 37.

cinematographic: used in *cinematography,* the art or technique of lighting and photography in making motion pictures. Page 19.

civil engineer: a person who designs public structures, such as roads, bridges, canals, dams and harbors, or supervises their construction or maintenance. Page 10.

claim-jumping: of or involved in *claim-jumping,* the seizing of another's claim, especially for mineral rights. *See also* **claim(s).** Page 92.

claim(s): a piece of land assigned to someone for purposes of removing minerals or other valuable substances, as by mining, drilling or the like. Page 28.

clannishness: a quality of being united together by some common trait, characteristic or interest; inclined to stick together as a close-knit group or family. Page 1.

cleat: a wooden or metal fitting, usually with two projecting horns, around which a rope may be secured. Page 108.

clodded field: an area of open ground covered with large lumps of earth. Page 61.

CMPE: an abbreviation for *Caribbean Motion Picture Expedition.* Page 26.

C.M.P. Expedition: also CMPE, an abbreviation for *Caribbean Motion Picture Expedition.* Page 25.

coast pilot: a manual published by a government for sailors, containing descriptions of coastal waters, harbor facilities, etc., for a specific area. A *pilot* in nautical terms is something serving as a guide through some unknown place or through a dangerous, difficult or unknown course. Page 10.

coffers: supplies or stores of money often belonging to a government or organization. From a box or chest, especially one for valuables or money. Page 29.

cogitation: the act or an instance of giving serious or deep thought (to something). Page 73.

coil: a device made of wire wound in spirals, used in an internal-combustion engine to increase the electrical force from the battery. The coil takes the relatively low electrical force of the battery and increases it to the extremely high force needed to make a spark in the spark plug. This spark is what ignites the fuel, causing the engine to run. Page 107.

College Park: a town near Washington, DC, established in 1745. The US Army Aviation School was established at the College Park Airfield in 1911 with aviation pioneer Wilbur Wright (1867–1912) as an instructor. The historic airport is the world's oldest in continuous operation. Page 50.

Columbia Pictures: a motion picture studio established in Hollywood, California, during the 1920s, becoming one of the largest US film companies. Page 91.

Columbus: Christopher Columbus (1451–1506), Italian explorer who sailed across the Atlantic Ocean in search of a westward sea route to Asia and was responsible for the European discovery of America in 1492. Page 29.

come out: end up in a certain state, position or the like. *Come out whole* means end up in one piece, undamaged or uninjured. Page 60.

commensurate: corresponding in extent or degree; proportionate. Page 100.

companion cockpit: an airplane cockpit designed so that the pilot and another person could sit beside each other, as in the Arrow Sport. *See also* **Arrow Sport.** Page 73.

complement: all the personnel that work on board a ship. Page 26.

concave: a curved recess, like the inner surface of a sphere; a depression resembling a bowl. Page 124.

confidant: a close, trusted friend. Page 9.

Congressional Airfield: an airport that was located near Washington, DC. It was the location of various flying schools and, in the early 1930s, was a site where LRH participated in stunt flying. Page 53.

Congressional hearing: a session held by a Congressional committee to gather information. (*Congressional* refers to *Congress,* the elected group of politicians responsible for making the law in the United States.) At such hearings, members of Congress listen to testimony from, and then direct questions to, witnesses such as government officials, experts and representatives of those affected by proposed laws under study. Information from such hearings forms the basis of committee reports or legislation. Page 84.

conk: fail suddenly in operation. Page 106.

Conquistadores: Spanish conquerors of Mexico and Peru in the sixteenth century. Page 29.

consummate: very skillful; complete. Page 113.

contrary: opposite in direction. For example, *contrary tides* are tides that flow in a direction opposite to the way a ship needs to travel. Page 20.

cooing: sounding overly sweet, friendly, charming or the like. Page 105.

Coolidge, Calvin: (1872–1933) thirtieth president of the United States (1923–1929). Page 4.

coolie: an unskilled worker, especially formerly in China or India. Page 35.

Corozal: a town in north central Puerto Rico. Page 29.

county fair: a *fair* is any of the annual outdoor events held in many parts of the United States with competitions for the best livestock, produce and prepared foods and with entertainment, rides and other amusements. A *county fair* is such an event held in a *county,* a unit of local government and one of the administrative subdivisions of a state in the US. Page 77.

cove(s): a small bay on the shore of the sea or a lake, especially one that is enclosed by high cliffs. Page 100.

coyote(s): a wild animal of the dog family, native to North America, distinguished from the wolf by its relatively small size and slender build, large ears and narrow muzzle. Page 2.

Crabtown: a nickname for Baltimore, Maryland, where crab from the Chesapeake Bay is a famous delicacy. Page 10.

cranked up: increased the speed of the aircraft engine, such as in order to take off. Page 73.

crate: an old, patched-up aircraft. Page 60.

cubic yard: a measurement of how many yards wide, tall and long something is. A *yard* is a unit of linear measure equal to 3 feet (36 inches or 0.9144 meter). Page 35.

cumin: a small herb native to the Mediterranean region, grown for its small seeds that have a strong, spicy taste. Page 112.

curators: persons in charge of a museum, art collection, etc. Page 120.

curio: any unusual or rare article; an unusual person. Page 73.

cutter: a sailboat with a single mast and one large triangular sail, often with one or more small triangular sails attached to or set forward of the mast. Page 106.

D.: (as noted on hand-drawn map) an abbreviation for *drift,* a horizontal or virtually horizontal mine shaft that follows a vein of ore. For example, the map of Drift No. 3 includes the label *D. 4.* This specifies the entrance (labeled *mouth*) to an adjoining drift, Drift No. 4. Page 32.

daisies, pushing: a slang expression meaning dead and in one's grave. Page 61.

damn the torpedoes: a reference to an exclamation made by American naval officer David Farragut (1801–1870), who won fame in a battle of the American Civil War (1861–1865). After witnessing another American ship sink after striking an explosive device floating near the surface of the water, called a torpedo at the time, Farragut shouted, "Damn the torpedoes! Full speed ahead!" and led his ships through to victory. Page 95.

Dare Devil(s): a person who is courageous and who takes risks, especially someone who performs dangerous stunts. Page 73.

daunted: lessened the courage of; disheartened. Page 61.

death on: dislike or oppose vigorously. Page 37.

decked: knocked to the ground with a punch. Page 9.

Department of Commerce: a department of the United States Government established in 1903 with the purpose to promote the nation's economic development and technological advancement. In 1926 the department included an Aeronautics Branch, which was responsible for regulating aviation facilities, air traffic rules, standards for those employed in aviation and the issuing of licenses, including pilots' licenses. Page 54.

derivative: using or taken from other sources; not original. Page 120.

devil, go-to-the-: demonstrating a carefree attitude. The allusion is to a well-designed glider, one that soars easily, completely disregarding gravity. Page 61.

Dianetics: Dianetics is a forerunner and substudy of Scientology. Dianetics means "through the mind" or "through the soul" (from Greek *dia,* through, and *nous,* mind or soul). It is a system of coordinated axioms which resolve problems concerning human behavior and psychosomatic illnesses. It combines a workable technique and a thoroughly validated method for increasing sanity, by erasing unwanted sensations and unpleasant emotions. Page 8.

distress pennant: a flag flown by a vessel to show that it is in danger or difficulty and needs help. Used figuratively. Page 25.

dive: a cheap, disreputable bar, gambling place, etc. Page 31.

Don: in Spanish-speaking countries, a gentleman; also a title (corresponding to Mr. or Sir) used in front of a man's first name. Page 32.

dope: a varnish applied to the cloth surface of airplane wings to increase strength and to keep them taut. Page 53.

double boiler: a pair of cooking pots, the upper one containing the food to be cooked and the lower one containing water that is heated. Page 112.

double-ended: having a similar appearance at both ends. Page 120.

dour: giving the impression of being unfriendly and severe. Page 20.

drift: a horizontal or virtually horizontal mine shaft that follows a vein of ore. Page 44.

drum up: bring about or obtain something through persistent effort. Page 41.

dual time: flying an airplane with an instructor. Page 85.

dunnage: personal baggage or belongings. Page 25.

du Pont, Dick: Richard Chichester du Pont (1911–1943), US businessman and aviator who was an early glider enthusiast. Page 57.

Eagle Scout: a Boy Scout who has reached the highest level of attainment in various tests of skill and endurance. The *Boy Scouts* are a worldwide organization founded in England in 1908 that teaches boys to be self-reliant, resourceful and courageous. Page 4.

ekes out: manages to make a living but only on a small scale and with a great deal of effort. Page 38.

element, into her: in the situation or environment for which the aircraft (she) is most suited, that is, the air. Page 77.

elevator: a hinged flap on the horizontal section of the tail of an aircraft, used to control the aircraft's up-and-down movement. Page 62.

end of, no: a great deal of something. Page 100.

epigrammatic: having or displaying an *epigram*, a concise saying or remark. Page 57.

escargot: an edible variety of snail. Page 111.

espiritismo: a form of spiritualism involving magic and communication with the spirits of the dead, along with traditional church rituals. Page 28.

ethnological: of or having to do with *ethnology*, the science that analyzes cultures, especially in regard to their historical development and the similarities and dissimilarities between them. Page 28.

ethnologist: someone trained and specializing in ethnology. *See also* **ethnological.** Page 100.

every man jack: every single person. *Jack* here means a common fellow or boy. Page 25.

Explorers Club: an organization, headquartered in New York and founded in 1904, devoted exclusively to promoting the science of exploration. To further this aim, it provides grants for those who wish to participate in field research projects and expeditions. It has provided logistical support for some of the twentieth century's most daring expeditions. L. Ron Hubbard was a lifetime member of the Explorers Club. Page 10.

Explorers Club flag: a flag awarded to active members of the Explorers Club who are in command of, or serving with, expeditions that further the cause of exploration and field science. Since 1918 the Explorers Club flag has been carried on hundreds of expeditions, including those to both North and South Poles, the summit of Mount Everest and the surface of the Moon. Many famous persons in history have carried the Explorers Club flag, including L. Ron Hubbard. Page 99.

Explorers Journal, The: a quarterly periodical published since 1921 by the Explorers Club. The club's *Journal* publishes articles and photographs from club members and others on expeditions across the globe. Page 117.

exponent: someone who promotes or speaks in favor of something. Page 35.

extraordinaire: outstanding in a particular capacity. Page 9.

factor in: include as an essential element, especially in planning something. Page 70.

Fairmile Class "B" Motor Launch: a World War II (1939–1945) patrol boat (launch) used in protecting coastal shipping and waterways from submarine threats, as well as in escort and rescue operations. The boat was a little over 100 feet long (30.48 meters) and was designed so that it could be rapidly reconfigured to fill different roles. Page 120.

fall: the loose end of a rope, as in *"make the other fall fast to the ship."* Page 106.

fall before the unknown: be ruined or defeated when facing something strange or unfamiliar, something that one knows nothing about. Page 1.

Farm Board: the Federal Farm Board, which was set up in the US in mid-1929 to help farmers. The Farm Board loaned money to *farm cooperatives,* businesses formed by farmers for collecting, marketing and selling their products jointly. The Farm Board also organized the purchase of farm surpluses. Both approaches were supposed to raise prices for agricultural products. Page 75.

farm relief: aid to farmers, as in the form of payments or the lifting of requirements to pay certain taxes, etc. Page 47.

fast, make: attach or tie firmly. Page 106.

fathom(s): a unit of length equal to 6 feet (1.8 meters), used chiefly in nautical measurements. Page 106.

fed up: an informal expression meaning bored with something, as from having had enough of it. Page 85.

feller: an informal way of saying *fellow,* a man. Page 61.

Fez: the third-largest city in Morocco. Founded in the late 700s, it has been a center of education, culture and religion for centuries. Page 111.

figured into: formed a key factor in something. Page 8.

Five-Novels Monthly: a pulp magazine published from 1928 until the late 1940s. The monthly schedule was continued until 1943, when paper shortages during World War II (1939–1945) forced it to a quarterly schedule and a resultant name change to *Five Novels* magazine. Page 54.

float: in mining, loose fragments of rock or ore (a metal-bearing mineral) that have been washed downhill and that are found in suspension, as in a river, or in the sand or gravel of the riverbed. Page 31.

flying jib: a small triangular sail that is the outermost sail projecting from the front of a ship. Page 21.

foresail: a large sail that is the principal sail on a *foremast,* the mast nearest the front of the ship. Page 21.

forlorn: deserted or abandoned and showing signs of neglect. Page 126.

Fort-de-France: the largest city on the island of Martinique and the capital since the late 1600s. Fort-de-France is located at a large bay in the southwestern end of the island. Page 20.

fountain of youth: a legendary spring of water that was supposed to make old people young. Early Spanish settlers in the Caribbean believed that the fountain was located on an island that, in 1513, Spanish explorer Juan Ponce de León set out to find. During his voyage he discovered Florida, which since then has been linked to the imaginary fountain. Page 41.

fragmentation: the pieces of an exploded *fragmentation bomb,* a bomb designed to break into many small, high-velocity fragments when detonated. Page 61.

Franklin PS2: a glider designed by Professor R. E. Franklin of the University of Michigan and built in 1929. *PS2* stands for "Primary and Secondary too," meaning it could use primary wings or the longer secondary wings interchangeably. *See also* **primary glider** and **secondary glider.** Page 53.

frijoles: beans cultivated and used for food, particularly in Mexico and in the southwestern United States. Page 110.

frontiersmen: men living on a frontier, especially in a newly pioneered territory of the United States. In early US history, frontiersmen were vital in the conquest of the land. Page 1.

fulminate (cap): a gray crystalline powder that explodes violently when struck or heated, used in detonators and in *percussion caps,* small, thin metal containers of explosive powder that are detonated to explode the main charge in a firearm. Page 94.

galleon: a large three-masted sailing ship used especially by the Spanish between the fifteenth and eighteenth centuries. Page 41.

gangue: worthless rock or other matter occurring in a vein or deposit within or alongside a valuable mineral. Page 44.

gassing facilities: facilities such as supply tanks, hoses, etc., for fueling aircraft with gas (petrol). Page 69.

gear: also *landing gear,* the wheels and related mechanisms used by an aircraft when taking off and landing. Page 73.

gentleman with the whiskers: a reference to *Father Time,* the personification of time as a bearded man of advanced years, usually wearing a robe and carrying a scythe and an hourglass. Page 60.

Geological Survey: the United States Geological Survey is the nation's largest water, earth science, biological science and civilian mapping agency. The Geological Survey collects, monitors, analyzes and provides scientific information about natural resource conditions, issues and problems. Page 10.

George Washington University: a private university, founded in 1821, in the city of Washington, DC. Named after the first president of the United States, George Washington (1732–1799), it maintains various schools of education, including the School of Engineering and Applied Science and the Columbian College of Arts and Sciences. The university has a long history of supporting research in physics and other technical fields. Page 10.

gesticulating: making or using gestures, especially in an animated or excited manner with or instead of speech. Page 38.

gibbet: an upright post with a beam projecting horizontally at the top, from which the bodies of criminals were hung and left on public display after execution. Page 41.

Gobi: a desert in northern China and southern Mongolia. The Gobi is the coldest and one of the largest deserts in the world. Page 100.

Goldwater, Barry: (1909–1998) American politician, United States senator from Arizona (1953–1965, 1969–1987) and Republican presidential candidate in 1964. Goldwater was noted as a conservative with strong views against Communism and an emphasis on maintaining US military strength. Page 110.

got about: became widely known, as in *"It got about the countryside, that afternoon."* Page 61.

go-to-the-devil: demonstrating a carefree attitude. The allusion is to a well-designed glider, one that soars easily, completely disregarding gravity. Page 61.

grace: be an attractive presence in or on, as by adding elegance, beauty, charm or the like. Page 38.

grace, fell from: lost the trust or respect that people have had (for one), especially by doing something wrong or immoral. Used humorously in the context of becoming an aviator. Page 84.

Great Depression: a drastic decline in the world economy starting in the United States, resulting in mass unemployment and widespread poverty that lasted from 1929 until 1939. Page 17.

Greco-Roman: having characteristics that are partly from ancient Greece and partly from ancient Rome; specifically, having the characteristics of Roman architecture or art done under strong Greek influence. Page 114.

grifter: a petty swindler, such as one who operates a dishonest gambling device at a carnival. Page 77.

groundlooping: making sudden unexpected sharp turns in an airplane on the ground in an effort to avoid something or because of loss of control. Page 77.

grubstake: supplies or money given to a prospector in return for a share in any profits from mining. Page 31.

Guam: an island in the northwestern Pacific Ocean, a territory of the United States and site of US air and naval bases. Page 1.

guidon: a small flag, broad at one end and pointed or forked at the other end, originally carried by the military for identification. Used figuratively. Page 131.

Gulf of Aden: a large body of water that runs along the southern shore of Yemen, where the city of Aden is located, south of Saudi Arabia. Page 120.

gummed: covered with a sticky (gummy) substance, as from the plants found in a swamp. Page 10.

gunnysacks: bags or sacks made of coarse, heavy fabric called *gunny*, also known as *burlap*. The sacks are typically used for transporting and storing grain, coffee, etc. Gunnysacks are also sometimes used as sandbags for erosion control. Page 33.

gunwales, to the: having much or too much of something; completely filled or filled to excess. Literally, *gunwales* means the top edge of a ship's sides that forms a ledge around the whole ship above the deck. Page 45.

Haidas: a Native North American people living along the coast of British Columbia in Canada, the adjoining Alaskan coast and the islands lying off these areas. Page 100.

Hammonds and Joplins: those like John Hammond and Harris Joplin, well-known American mining engineers of the late 1800s and early 1900s. Page 31.

hand called, have (one's): have (one's) statements questioned to find out the source of (one's) information. From the game of poker, in reference to a call for each player to lay down his hand (the cards he is holding) face up so everyone can see who is holding which cards and the winner can be determined. Page 94.

hapless: unlucky; unfortunate. Page 19.

Hartford, Conn.: a city in and the capital of Connecticut, a state in the northeastern United States. Page 26.

Hartford Radio Relay League: an organization of amateur radio operators, founded in 1914 in Hartford, Connecticut. With amateur radio operators in many different parts of the United States, the league was able to transmit messages by relaying from one member to another. As the American Radio Relay League, the group subsequently grew into the largest organization for amateur radio enthusiasts in the US. Page 26.

hatch: the covering over an opening in the deck that leads to a lower area. Page 107.

haunts: places frequently visited. Page 17.

Hawks, Frank: (1897–1938) aviation pioneer who set numerous speed records, such as his 1930 transcontinental flight from Los Angeles to New York City in twelve hours and twenty-five minutes. Page 53.

heady: having a strong or exhilarating effect. Page 111.

heathens: persons who do not belong to a widely held religion (especially Christianity, Judaism or Islam), as regarded by those who do. Page 40.

heel(ing): lean over to one side. Page 107.

heels of, on the: closely following; just after. Page 53.

helm: the wheel or handle that controls the direction in which a ship or boat travels. Page 20.

Henry, O.: pen name of William Sydney Porter (1862–1910), American short-story writer noted for his mastery of plot twists that build to an unexpected ending. Page 47.

high-faller: a *faller* is a logger who cuts down trees. A *high-faller* is another name for a *high-rigger*. *See also* **high-rigger.** Page 93.

high-rigger: also called *high-faller,* one who climbs very tall trees, chopping off lower branches as he climbs, and then chops off the top of the tree. The straight trunks of such trees can be used to set up (rig) the cables (heavy wire rope) used in moving cut trees out of a forest and to a landing site for shipping. Cables mounted high above the ground allow cut trees to be moved over the tops of standing trees to the landing site. *See also* **high-faller.** Page 93.

high-tension: *tension* in this sense is a synonym for *voltage,* the amount of pressure or force behind an electrical flow. *High-tension wires* are electrical power lines designed for carrying large amounts of voltage, usually found well off the ground, strung across a series of poles, one after another. Page 70.

Hillary, Edmund: Edmund Percival Hillary (1919–2008), a New Zealand mountain climber and explorer who became one of the first two men to reach the top of Mount Everest, the world's tallest mountain, and return. On 29 May 1953, he and Tenzing Norgay, a mountain climber from Nepal, reached the 29,035-foot (8,850-meter) summit. Page 100.

hillman: of or relating to people who are native to or inhabiting a hilly or mountainous, often isolated, area and typically differing markedly in outlook, customs and speech from people of the plains. Used here in reference to the *jíbaros* of Puerto Rico. Page 32.

hinterland: an area far from big cities and towns. Page 28.

hobnails: large-headed nails on the soles of heavy boots and shoes that protect the soles. Page 49.

honey-comb quartz: *quartz,* a brilliant, crystalline mineral, often found in conjunction with gold. Some forms of quartz appear as crystals in which each crystal has six sides, like the individual cells of a honey-comb (a wax structure made by bees to store honey and eggs). Page 38.

horn, like notes through the: like musical tones thought of as winding around and around and finally out of a *horn,* a wind instrument usually made of brass and consisting of a long tube with a flared end that produces a sound when the player's lips vibrate together into the mouthpiece. Page 64.

hot dawg: representing an informal pronunciation of *hot dog,* an expression indicating great joy or delight. Page 63.

Hydrographic Office: a section of the Department of the Navy charged with making hydrographic surveys and publishing charts and other information for naval and commercial vessels, information key to national defense. *Hydrographic* means of or relating to the scientific charting, description and analysis of the physical conditions, boundaries and flow of oceans, lakes, rivers, etc. Page 100.

iguana: a large plant-eating tropical lizard, chiefly found in South and Central America. Page 110.

Iliad: one of the oldest surviving Greek poems, dating from the 700s B.C. The *Iliad* describes certain events in the final year of the Trojan War, which was fought between Greece and the city of Troy, a war that, according to legend, ended with the defeat of Troy by the Greeks. Many scholars believe the legend is based on a real war of the mid-1200s B.C. Page 118.

illusive: having qualities of an *illusion,* as in being thought of as unreal, imaginary or the like. Page 29.

incarnation(s): each of a series of earthly lifetimes or forms. Page 118.

Incas: a Native South American people whose huge empire flourished from the twelfth century A.D. until the mid-sixteenth century. Page 41.

incited: stimulated or prompted to action. Page 100.

indigenous: originating in and characteristic of a particular region or country; native. Page 100.

indiscreet: without good judgment; not carefully restrained; unwise. Page 45.

indolent: marked by a dislike or avoidance of work; idle; lazy. Page 32.

innocent of: completely lacking (in something, such as a particular substance, quality or the like). Page 36.

Inside Passage: a natural protected waterway in northwestern North America, 950 miles (1,500 kilometers) long. It extends along the coast from Seattle, Washington, USA, past British Columbia, Canada, to the southern area of Alaska. The passage is made up of a series of channels running between the mainland and a string of islands on the west that protect the passage from Pacific Ocean storms. Page 100.

in tow: in the state of being *towed,* pulled along by another vehicle. Page 62.

iron horse: a slang term for a *locomotive,* an engine that pulls a railroad train. Page 25.

irons, in: imprisoned with metal chains or bands around the legs or arms. Page 25.

irony: a combination of circumstances or a result that is the opposite of what is or might be expected. Page 100.

jack, every man: every single person. *Jack* here means a common fellow or boy. Page 25.

Jamaica: an island nation in the Caribbean Sea, about 480 miles (772 kilometers) south of Florida. A popular tourist destination, Jamaica is the third-largest island in the Caribbean. The country became independent in 1962, having been a colony of Great Britain since the late 1600s. Page 17.

jibaro: a person from a rural area of Puerto Rico. Page 28.

johnny cake: a cake or bread made of cornmeal and water or milk, usually cooked on a griddle (a heavy, flat, metal plate or pan for cooking on). Page 10.

joy riders, Sunday: people taking a pleasure drive on a Sunday. Page 61.

keel: the long piece of wood or steel along the bottom of a boat that forms the major part of its structure and helps to keep the boat balanced in the water. Page 118.

keeps, for: with serious intent or purpose. Page 77.

keep the tongue away from the cheek: mean something seriously, the opposite of the phrase *tongue in cheek,* intended as a joke, as if one were putting one's tongue in one's cheek while saying something, a gesture indicating that the remark is not meant seriously. Here used with a pun on *tongue,* in reference to the cows licking the wings of the plane. Page 79.

Kentland: a town in Illinois, a state in the north central United States. Page 77.

ketch: a two-masted sailing boat with sails set lengthwise (fore and aft) and with the mast closer to the front taller than the mast behind. Page 100.

kimono, wooden: a humorous reference to a glider, the main building material being wood and cloth and, with its wings, somewhat resembling a *kimono,* a Japanese floor-length garment with wide sleeves. Page 61.

kindling: dry split wood suitable for lighting fires. Page 95.

Kodiak bear: a large brown bear inhabiting Kodiak Island (off the southwestern coast of Alaska) as well as coastal areas of Alaska and the west coast of Canada. Also called *Kodiak,* this bear can grow to a height of 9 feet (2.7 meters) and can attain a weight of around 1,700 pounds (780 kilograms). Page 100.

Kuril Islands: a chain of fifty-six large and small volcanic islands off the northeastern coast of Asia, extending from northern Japan to a southern peninsula in Russia. Page 100.

Lady Luck, Old: luck (chance considered as a force causing success or failure), thought of as a lady who brings a person either good luck or bad luck. Page 60.

Lafayette Escadrille: during World War I (1914–1918), a group of American volunteers who flew with the French air force from 1915 to 1917. From *escadrille,* the French word for squadron, and *Lafayette,* a reference to the Marquis de Lafayette (1757–1834), French military leader and nobleman remembered as a hero for his help in achieving American independence. He fought for the United States during the American Revolution (1775–1783), holding high positions in the army and working closely with George Washington. Page 69.

laid (oneself) open to: made (oneself) liable or exposed to something. Page 95.

lamaseries: monasteries of *lamas,* priests or monks of a branch of Buddhism that is practiced in certain areas of China. Page 8.

lamprey casserole: a stew or other moist food dish consisting of *lamprey,* a fish with an eellike body, baked usually with rice, potatoes or macaroni. Page 110.

landlubber: an informal term for a person who has had little experience at sea or who is unfamiliar with the sea or sailing. Page 26.

Las Palmas: a seaport in and capital of the Canary Islands. *See also* **Canary Islands.** Page 122.

lath: a thin, narrow, flat piece of wood used to form a frame for support of plasterwork in building a wall, ceiling, etc. Page 107.

latitude: the distance measured in degrees of angle of a point on the Earth's surface north or south of the equator. The North Pole is 90 degrees north; the South Pole is 90 degrees south. Latitude along with longitude is used to determine location. Page 28.

layout: a set of something such as clothing, equipment or the like. Page 25.

leading edge: the forward edge of an aircraft wing, specifically in reference to a single wing mounted on top of the fuselage of the glider. With the pilot sitting in an open cockpit, the wing was just behind and above the cockpit. Page 54.

league: 1. an older measurement of distance of variable length, usually about 3 miles (5 kilometers). Page 20.
2. an association, as of people, groups or the like, with common interests or goals, that combine for mutual cooperation. Page 26.

leasing: the making of a legal agreement by which money is paid to use something, such as equipment, a vehicle or the like, for an agreed period of time. Hence a *leasing agent* is an agent (a person who organizes transactions between two other parties) who sees that equipment owned by one person is leased to another who wishes to use the equipment for a specified period of time. Page 19.

LeBlond: an aircraft engine built by LeBlond Engines of Cincinnati, Ohio, used in small aircraft of the 1920s and 1930s and capable of producing 60 horsepower. Page 69.

Lesser Antilles: islands of the West Indies that extend in an arc from Puerto Rico to the northeastern coast of South America, including Dominica, Grenada, Saint Lucia, Saint Vincent, Martinique, Saint Kitts, Antigua and the Virgin Islands. Page 20.

Lindbergh: Charles Augustus Lindbergh (1902–1974), American aviator and engineer, known for being the first person to make a nonstop solo flight across the Atlantic. Page 53.

list: an instance of leaning over to one side. A *"forty-five degree list"* means leaning at an angle that is halfway between horizontal and vertical. Page 61.

live-wire: an energetic, alert person. Page 31.

Livingstone: David Livingstone (1813–1873), Scottish missionary and physician who explored southern and central Africa. Page 117.

lode: an amount of valuable metal, such as gold, silver or the like, in its natural form. Page 28.

longitude: the distance measured in degrees of angle of a point on the Earth's surface east or west of a line that runs from the North Pole to the South Pole through Greenwich, England. A circle (the Earth) is 360 degrees—lines of longitude run from 0 (line through Greenwich) to 180 degrees east (E) and from 0 (line through Greenwich) to 180 degrees west (W). Longitude along with latitude is used to determine location.

Long Table: the famous table at the Explorers Club in New York where members have traditionally gathered to entertain one another with stories of their adventures. *See also* **Explorers Club.** Page 103.

LORAN: a system by which the position of a ship or aircraft can be determined by the time interval between radio signals received from two or more known stations. The term is derived from *LO*ng *RA*nge *N*avigation. Page 100.

lost Canadian border: a reference to a 1931 United States Geological Survey team of which L. Ron Hubbard was a member. The team was to locate damaged or destroyed US/Canada border markers in the northeastern state of Maine to settle the geographic limit of the United States. Page 10.

lowering: having a dark and threatening look. Page 40.

Lucky Lindy: nickname of Charles Augustus Lindbergh (1902–1974), American aviator and engineer. He was given the nickname by the press after his 1927 achievement of being the first person to fly solo nonstop across the Atlantic. Page 53.

Mac: a nickname used for someone with a last name that starts with Mc or Mac. Specifically, in the context, the name is McBride. Page 43.

machete: a large heavy knife used especially in Latin American countries in cutting sugar cane and clearing underbrush (undergrowth in a forest) and as a weapon. Page 37.

mags: a shortening of *magnetos,* small alternators (devices that generate alternating current) that use permanent magnets to generate a spark in an internal-combustion engine, especially in marine and aircraft engines. Page 77.

Maine: the northernmost state on the east coast of the United States. Page 10.

make fast: attach or tie firmly. Page 106.

mañana: an indefinite time in the future. *Mañana* is Spanish for *tomorrow*. Page 43.

Manchuria: a region of northeastern China. Page 9.

manganese: a hard, brittle, grayish-white metallic element, used chiefly in steel to give it toughness. Page 28.

Mann, Bill: William M. Mann (1886–1960), director of the National Zoo in Washington, DC. During his thirty years as director of the National Zoo (1925–1955), Mann was responsible for building up and expanding the zoo facilities while fitting in travel to distant places in search of animals to add to the collection. Page 103.

Marine Corps: a branch of the United States armed forces trained for land, sea and air combat, typically landing near a battle zone either from the air or from a ship. Page 54.

Marines, 20th: a reserve unit of the Marine Corps. Page 10.

marjoram: a fragrant and aromatic mint used as seasoning in cookery. Page 111.

Martinique: an island in the West Indies (a group of islands in the Atlantic between North and South America). It was colonized by French settlers after 1635. Page 17.

Maryland: a state in the eastern United States on the Atlantic coast, surrounding Washington, DC, on all but one side. Page 45.

Med: short for *Mediterranean Sea,* the sea lying between Europe, Africa and Asia. Page 112.

medicine man: among Native North American peoples, someone believed to have supernatural powers of curing disease and controlling spirits. Page 2.

mesmerism: compelling attraction; fascination. Page 53.

"metallic sunshine": a term used to describe gold. From *metallic,* of or consisting of metal; also, shiny and highly reflective. And *sunshine,* the sun's light and, figuratively, something with the bright, cheerful, prosperous look or quality suggestive of sunshine. Page 28.

mete out: deal out or give out, as punishment. Page 37.

Michigan: a state in the north central United States. Page 17.

Middle West: the northern region of the central United States east of the Rocky Mountains. The area is known for its rich farmlands. Page 73.

midway: at a fair or carnival, the place or area on which sideshows and similar amusements are located. Page 77.

minded: objected to; disliked. Page 43.

mineralized: containing mineral substances. Page 44.

Mitchell, Edgar: Edgar Dean Mitchell (1930–), American astronaut, member of the *Apollo 14* mission (Jan–Feb 1971) and the sixth person to walk on the Moon. Mitchell retired from the space program in 1972. Interested in parapsychology, he founded the Institute of Noetic (of inner knowing) Sciences in Palo Alto, California. Page 118.

m'lord: a contraction of *milord,* also *my lord,* a term of address for a young English nobleman. Used humorously in reference to the men sailing aboard the *Doris Hamlin*. Page 25.

Model A: an automobile introduced by the Ford Motor Company in 1927 to replace their earlier Model T. More powerful than the Model T, the Model A was an attractive vehicle produced in several body styles and in a choice of four colors. Ford produced half a million Model As until they were discontinued in the early 1930s. Page 61.

Model T: an automobile manufactured by the Ford Motor Company, the first motor vehicle successfully mass-produced on an assembly line. Model Ts were produced between 1908 and 1927. Also used to refer to anything considered old and out-of-date. Page 4.

Montana: a state in the northwestern United States bordering on Canada. Page 2.

Mother Hubbard: a long, loose-fitting, shapeless dress, named for a nursery rhyme character who was depicted wearing such. Page 42.

mother lode: the main deposit, or vein, of gold in a particular region or district. Page 36.

muslin: a type of firm cloth, usually made of cotton. Page 60.

mustachios: a thick or fancy mustache, often trimmed into a fancy shape. Page 35.

n

nabbed: an informal term meaning caught or arrested a criminal or wrongdoer. Page 100.

Nan-k'ou Pass: an opening through the Nan-k'ou mountain range in China about 50 miles (80 kilometers) north of Beijing (formerly Peking). The pass is the site of a fortified section of China's Great Wall, well known as the location of battles against invading tribes. A railway, linking Beijing to areas in the north, runs through the pass and through a gateway in the Great Wall itself. Page 10.

National Archives: an agency of the United States Government that has the purpose to select, preserve and make historically valuable government records available to the federal government and the public. Page 10.

National Guard: in the United States, the military forces of the individual states, which can be called into active service for emergencies, for national defense, as a police force or the like. Page 8.

National Museum: the United States National Museum, located in Washington, DC, which includes major collections of American history and technology, and natural history. The National Museum is administered by the *Smithsonian Institution,* a group of scientific and cultural institutes created in 1846 from a grant given by British scientist James Smithson. Page 23.

Nebraska: a state in the central part of the United States. Page 2.

nether regions: a region imagined as lying beneath the Earth; the place inhabited by the souls of the dead; Hell. Page 23.

Nevada: a state in the western part of the United States. Page 2.

New London: a town in northern Ohio, a state in the north central United States. Page 79.

Newport, Indiana: a town about 50 miles (80 kilometers) west of Indianapolis, the capital of Indiana, a state in the north central United States. Page 77.

newsreel: a short cinema film dealing with news and current affairs. Page 17.

Newton's law: a reference to mathematician Sir Isaac Newton's (1642–1727) Law of Universal Gravitation, which states that a falling mass increases in speed as it moves toward Earth. Page 62.

New York Times: a daily newspaper published in New York City since 1851 and, today, distributed nationally. Page 23.

nitroglycerin: a highly explosive chemical compound, very sensitive to shock and liable to explode if jarred suddenly. Page 92.

nominal: very small in comparison with the real cost or value. Page 69.

Nora: a site in southern Sardinia, the location of ancient ruins from Roman and earlier civilizations, some as early as the eighth century B.C. Page 118.

North Sea: the arm of the Atlantic Ocean lying between the eastern coast of Great Britain and the continent of Europe. Page 120.

notes through the horn, like: like musical tones thought of as winding around and around and finally out of a *horn,* a wind instrument usually made of brass and consisting of a long tube with a flared end that produces a sound when the player's lips vibrate together into the mouthpiece. Page 64.

off chance, on the: in or with the slight hope or possibility; just in case something happens. Page 118.

Oklahoma: a state in the south central part of the United States. Page 2.

Old Lady Luck: luck (chance considered as a force causing success or failure), thought of as a lady who brings a person either good luck or bad luck. Page 60.

O'Meara, Jack: John K. (Jack) O'Meara (1909?–1941), one of the top US glider pilots of the 1930s, well known for setting numerous records for glider flights. Page 57.

Orientalist: a person who studies the cultures of the East, such as in the countries of China, Japan and India. Page 10.

Orlando, Cape: a point on the northern coast of Sicily, near the eastern end of the island. Page 122.

outcrop(s): a large area of rock sticking out of the ground. Page 47.

palm (someone): touch or catch (someone). Page 62.

Panhandle: part of the state of Alaska that extends along the Pacific coast, south from the main part of the state. A *panhandle* is a narrow section of land shaped like the handle of a cooking pan, that extends away from the body of the state it belongs to. Page 100.

pan, sluicing: also *mining pan,* an open container for washing out gold, tin, etc., from gravel or the like, in mining. Page 36.

Pa. RR: an abbreviation for *Pennsylvania Railroad. See also* **Pennsylvania Railroad.** Page 25.

passageway: also *passage,* a narrow body of water between two land masses, which is a route or channel that ships may sail along. Page 106.

peg: throw, especially low and fast. Page 109.

Pegasus: an aircraft engine built in England by the Bristol Aeroplane Company. A powerful engine, the Pegasus was capable of producing several hundred horsepower. A "pony Pegasus" is an allusion to a small engine, for example, the 60-horsepower LeBlond engine that powered the Arrow Sport. (*Pegasus* is the name of the winged horse in Greek myths.) *See also* **Arrow Sport** and **LeBlond.** Page 75.

Peking: former name of Beijing, the capital of China. Page 8.

Pelée: a volcano in the West Indies, on the island of Martinique. Page 21.

Pennsylvania Railroad: a major American railroad transportation system in the eastern part of the United States. Page 25.

pernicious: having a very harmful effect; destructive. Page 43.

per se: by or in itself, essentially; without reference to anything else. Page 1.

Phoenician: of or relating to *Phoenicia,* an ancient kingdom at the eastern end of the Mediterranean Sea, in the region of present-day Syria, Lebanon and Israel. Page 122.

piano wire: a special kind of strong steel wire used for the strings of pianos. Page 53.

pike pole: a long pole, at one end of which is a *pike,* a sharp iron or steel point. Page 108.

pilothouse: an enclosed structure on the deck of a boat or ship containing navigating equipment, charts and the like and from which the vessel can be navigated. Page 107.

pimento: a hot, spicy pepper that is dried and crushed and used in cooking. Page 111.

pitchy: full of sap (pitch) that comes from the bark of pine trees. Page 95.

Pizarro: Francisco Pizarro (1474?–1541), Spanish explorer and soldier who set out on an expedition to colonize Peru for Spain. In 1531 he and his two partners landed in Peru with about one hundred and eighty men, some cannons and horses. The Incas (rulers of a vast empire in South America) had a civilization wealthy in gold, silver and other natural resources, but they were already divided by a civil war when Pizarro arrived, so he easily defeated the army of the Inca ruler. Page 41.

placer: a deposit of sand or gravel found, for example, in the bed of a stream, containing particles of gold or some other valuable mineral. A placer deposit is washed to separate valuable minerals. Page 42.

plumed: decorated with a *plume,* a large feather or group of feathers worn on a hat. Page 41.

Podunk: a fictitious small country village or town (thought of as insignificant and out of contact with the progress of the world). Page 70.

Ponce de León: Juan Ponce de León (1460?–1521), Spanish explorer who accompanied Christopher Columbus on his second voyage to America. Ponce de León became governor of the island of Puerto Rico in the early 1500s. His explorations of Florida were aimed at discovering the fountain of youth. Page 41.

port: a small round window or opening in the side or other exterior part of a ship, for admitting light or air. Also called a *porthole*. Page 107.

Port Huron: a city and port at the southern tip of Lake Huron in southeastern Michigan, a state in the north central United States. Page 17.

port(s) of call: a harbor town or city where ships can visit during the course of a voyage. Page 17.

potentate: a person having great power and authority; one who rules over others; ruler. Page 38.

potpourri: a miscellaneous mixture of things. Page 110.

power(less) ship: a *ship* in this context is an aircraft, such as an airplane or glider. A *power ship*, such as an airplane, has an engine. A *powerless ship*, such as a glider, has no engine. Page 53.

Pratt Street: a street in Baltimore, Maryland, near the docks. Page 25.

precariously: in a manner that is dependent upon chance or circumstances; in a way that is uncertain or insecure. Page 53.

prefatory: serving to introduce something else, such as a main body of text. Page 103.

prelude: 1. an action or event coming before and introducing another. Page 4.
2. act as an introduction to something else. Page 113.

primary glider: a ruggedly built glider used for training glider pilots. Page 54.

primary's: belonging to a *primary glider. See also* **primary glider.** Page 53.

privation: lack of what is needed for existence; hardship. Page 105.

progenitor(s): someone who develops something; an originator. Page 25.

prop: an informal term for an aircraft propeller. Page 73.

prosaic: belonging to or suitable for the everyday world; commonplace; down-to-earth. Page 122.

Puerto Rico: a self-governing island in the northern Caribbean Sea, associated with the United States since its acquisition from Spain in 1898. Also part of Puerto Rico are two islands off the east coast, Vieques and Culebra. Puerto Rico is located 1,000 miles (1,600 kilometers) southeast of Florida and about 600 miles (965 kilometers) north of Caracas, Venezuela. Page 17.

Puget Sound: a long, narrow bay of the Pacific Ocean on the coast of Washington, a state in the northwestern United States. Page 92.

Purdue: a reference to *Purdue University,* located in Indiana and founded in 1869. Page 77.

purgatory: in Roman Catholic doctrine, the place in which the souls remain until they have made up for their sins before they go to heaven. Page 45.

pursuit job: a fighter plane designed for pursuit of and attack on enemy airplanes. (*Job* is a term used to describe something that is manufactured, such as a motor vehicle or aircraft.) Page 84.

pushrod: a metal rod in an internal-combustion engine that is part of the linkage used to open and close the *valves,* devices that control the movement of fuel and air into the engine. Page 77.

quartet: literally, a group of four singers or musicians. Used figuratively to describe something that sounds like a quartet of machine guns. Page 77.

quartz, honey-comb: *quartz,* a brilliant, crystalline mineral, often found in conjunction with gold. Some forms of quartz appear as crystals in which each crystal has six sides, like the individual cells of a honey-comb (a wax structure made by bees to store honey and eggs). Page 38.

quinine: a powerful drug with a bitter taste. Primarily used for relief of pain and fevers, quinine was once the only treatment available for malaria. However, due to its disturbing side effects, it has largely been replaced by other drugs. Page 28.

quipped: made a clever or witty comment. Page 2.

ramshackle: poorly maintained or constructed and seeming likely to fall apart or collapse. Page 31.

range broncs, breaking: taming wild or partly tamed horses of the range (large area of open land, as in the western United States) to a point where they can be saddled and ridden without trying to throw off riders. Page 2.

Red Sea: a sea between northeastern Africa and western Arabia. Page 120.

reformatory: an institution to which young people who break the law are sent to reform (correct and improve fault in one's conduct or character). Page 37.

regalia: the distinctive clothing worn by a particular group of people. Page 43.

replete (with): including or having something. Page 100.

Rickenbacker, Eddie: (1890–1973) American aviator and the leading American combat pilot in World War I (1914–1918). He served in the *United States Air Service,* a branch of the US Army and forerunner of the US Air Force. As a member and later commanding officer of the 94th Aero

Pursuit Squadron, Rickenbacker shot down twenty-two enemy planes and was decorated by both the US and French governments for his service. Page 69.

ride, taken for a: subjected to teasing. Page 93.

riffles: in mining, slats or bars laid on the bottom of a sluice to form a series of grooves or open spaces for catching and holding particles of gold. Page 33.

rifts: flat, even surfaces; levels. Page 82.

Río Negro: a river in Puerto Rico. *Río* is the Spanish word for river. Page 33.

Rockies: short for the *Rocky Mountains*. *See also* **Rocky Mountains**. Page 44.

Rocky Mountains: major mountain system of western North America, extending approximately 3,000 miles (4,800 kilometers) through the United States and Canada. The width of the system varies from 70 to 400 miles (110 to 650 kilometers) and the elevation from 5,000 feet (1,500 meters) to 14,433 feet (4,399 meters) at Mount Elbert, Colorado, the highest point in the Rockies. Page 4.

romance: a spirit or feeling of adventure, excitement and the potential for heroic achievement. Page 69.

Roman Empire: the empire of ancient Rome (which at its peak included western and southern Europe, Britain, North Africa and the lands of the eastern Mediterranean Sea) that lasted from 27 B.C. to A.D. 476, when it fell to invading Germanic tribes. Page 124.

rotisserie: a method of cooking by turning slowly over a fire or other source of heat. Page 110.

roughneck: a member of a crew that builds and repairs oil wells. Page 93.

roughriding: characteristic of a *roughrider*, literally, someone who breaks wild horses (trains them so they can be ridden) or who is used to rough or hard riding, as over difficult terrain. Used figuratively to describe someone having an active, aggressive attitude, someone who is used to dealing with problems energetically. Page 110.

roughshod, ride: pay no attention to (something that could be in the way); disregard. Page 95.

roustabout: a workman in an *oil field,* an area having valuable deposits of petroleum, often one with a number of active oil wells. Page 92.

rover(s): someone who goes from place to place, never having a particular course or destination and never settling anywhere for long. Page 26.

roving: traveling over an assigned route, as in gathering news stories. Page 54.

running board: a small ledge or step, formerly beneath the doors of an automobile, to assist passengers entering or leaving the car. Page 77.

running bowline: a type of knot that forms a noose with the knot below the opening of the loop. The noose can then be thrown over something that is out of reach. Page 106.

Ryan ST: an airplane designed by Tubal Claude Ryan (1898–1982), American aviator and aircraft manufacturer. The Ryan ST was used by the army as its basic training plane, the PT-22. (*ST* stands for *Sport Trainer* and *PT* stands for *Primary Trainer*.) *See also* **Ryan, T. Claude.** Page 84.

Ryan, T. Claude: Tubal Claude Ryan (1898–1982), American aviator and aircraft manufacturer. Ryan began flying in 1917 and through the years was responsible for notable advances in design and manufacture of airplanes. As head of Ryan Airlines during the mid-1920s, he flew passengers between San Diego and Los Angeles and also built American aviator Charles Lindbergh's plane, *Spirit of St. Louis*. Starting another company in 1929, he designed the Ryan ST. *See also* **Ryan ST** and *Spirit of St. Louis.* Page 84.

saber: a light sword with a guard to cover the hand and a tapering flexible blade, used in fencing. Page 9.

saffron: an orange-yellow spice used for flavoring and coloring food. Page 112.

sage: a bushy plant native to Mediterranean areas and whose leaves and stems are used as a seasoning. Page 111.

sailplane: another term for a *glider*, a heavier-than-air aircraft without an engine. Page 84.

Saint-Pierre: a town founded in 1635 on Martinique, an island in the Caribbean Sea. It was once the largest and most important community on the island, a major export center for rum, molasses and sugar. In 1902, the hot gas and ashes of erupting Mount Pelée destroyed the town, killing all but one of its thirty thousand inhabitants. Page 21.

salty: associated with the sea or with nautical life. Page 25.

sample pick: a type of lightweight, hand-held pick used by prospectors and miners in taking samples, often having a square head on one end for hammering into surfaces and a pointed tip on the other end for breaking up ore. Taking samples involves striking off bits of rock along a rock face, collecting the bits and then having them analyzed to determine their mineral content. Page 28.

San Diego: a city and seaport in southwestern California, the second-largest city in the state (after Los Angeles). Page 4.

San Germán: a town in the southwestern part of Puerto Rico. One of the earliest Spanish communities on the island, San Germán was founded in the early 1500s. Page 44.

San Juan: the principal seaport and capital of Puerto Rico. *See also* **Puerto Rico.** Page 28.

Sardinia: an Italian island in the Mediterranean Sea. It is the second-largest island in the Mediterranean after Sicily. Page 114.

Sargasso Sea: an irregular oval-shaped area of the western North Atlantic Ocean, northeast of the Caribbean, whose boundaries are defined by four ocean currents. Inside these currents, the waters of the Sargasso are calmer, warmer and more salty than the waters of the flowing currents. The name comes from the brown seaweed that floats in massive clumps on the still surface of the water. Page 20.

savvy: knowledge and experience. Page 43.

Schliemann, Heinrich: (1822–1890) German archaeologist who excavated ancient cities in Greece and Turkey, including the ruins of Troy. Page 118.

schooner: a sailing ship with sails set lengthwise (fore and aft) and having from two to as many as seven masts. Page 8.

Schwartz, Stephan A.: a researcher and author in parapsychology who has worked with a number of research laboratories, including the Rhine Research Center, founded by American psychologist Joseph Banks Rhine (1895–1980). Page 120.

Scientology: Scientology is the study and handling of the spirit in relationship to itself, universes and other life. The term Scientology is taken from the Latin *scio,* which means "knowing in the fullest sense of the word," and the Greek word *logos,* meaning "study of." In itself the word means literally "knowing how to know." Page 1.

scour (something) down: literally, move rapidly through an area. Used figuratively to mean move rapidly through something, such as data or information, as in telling about an incident. Page 45.

Scouting: the activities of the *Boy Scouts,* a worldwide organization founded in England in 1908 that instructs in practical skills and teaches boys to be self-reliant, resourceful and courageous. Page 7.

scurried: moved quickly. Page 45.

scuttled: ran or moved hurriedly with short, quick steps. Page 108.

seat of one's pants, fly by the: to handle an airplane by instinct or from experience. This expression originates from the early days of aviation when airplanes had few, if any, instruments. Pilots had to rely upon instinct based on experience rather than technical aids. Page 53.

secondary glider: the *secondary glider,* or *sailplane,* is built like an ordinary airplane and has a cockpit for seating one to two people. The wings are longer than those on a primary glider. Overall, secondary gliders are designed for aerodynamic efficiency. *Aerodynamic* means relating to the characteristics of the outer body of an aircraft that affect the performance with which it moves through the air. Page 84.

second-hand: used or worn, as from previous usage; hence poor condition. Page 45.

Secret of Treasure Island, The: the series of films produced by Columbia Pictures, drawn from the L. Ron Hubbard novel *Murder at Pirate Castle.* LRH's screenplays for the serial, written during 1937, became a box office success. Page 91.

see (one) through: provide (someone) with help or support for a particular period of time. Page 4.

sepulcher(s): a tomb, grave or burial place. Page 124.

serial: any of the short movies shown as a series of up to fifteen separate installments, often in conjunction with a full-length film. These short films, each with a dramatic ending, drew the audience back each week for the next exciting chapter in the story. Page 91.

serviette: a square of cloth, generally used as a table napkin and also functioning to wrap foods for cooking. Page 112.

72nd Street: in New York City, the original location of the Explorers Club, which is now a few blocks away at 70th Street, between Park Avenue and Madison Avenue. This section of New York City, known as the Upper East Side, is one of the most prestigious areas of the city. Page 99.

shashlik: a type of shish kebab, the shashlik (a Russian word) uses lamb that has been soaked for several hours in a *marinade,* a liquid such as wine or vinegar seasoned with herbs. *See also* **shish kebab.** Page 112.

ship, (power, powerless): a *ship* in this context is an aircraft, such as an airplane or glider. A *power ship,* such as an airplane, has an engine. A *powerless ship,* such as a glider, has no engine. Page 53.

shirtwaist: a woman's blouse (or part of a dress from the waist up) that resembles the style of a man's shirt. Page 43.

shish kebab: a dish consisting of small pieces of meat and vegetables that have been put on a long thin stick or metal rod and cooked together. Page 112.

shock cord: a cord made of rubber strands bound in woven casing, designed to absorb or resist shock, as from impacts. Shock cords have been used to tow gliders as a way of launching them, as landing shock absorbers on small airplanes and for other aviation uses. Page 53.

shooter: a person who sets off explosives in oil-drilling operations. Page 92.

shoots: causes (an amount of explosives) to blow up. Page 94.

shot level: moved or caused something to move quickly and suddenly into a level position, that is, a position of being parallel with the ground. Page 60.

Sicily: largest island in the Mediterranean, Sicily is a region of Italy, located off the southwestern tip of the mainland. Page 122.

signal: notably out of the ordinary; remarkable; outstanding. Page 100.

signaling: transmitting messages over a long distance, such as by means of blinking lights, buzzers, flags or the like. Signaling includes the use of codes to represent letters of the alphabet, such as long and short lights or sounds, or holding flags in different positions. Page 7.

silicon: an abundant, brittle nonmetallic chemical element found naturally in sand, granite, clay and in many minerals. Page 28.

simmered (something) down to: simplified or summarized to a certain number, amount or the like. *Simmer down* refers to the action of reducing the bulk of something by cooking at a temperature just below the boiling point, hence to make more condensed by elimination of that which can be spared. Page 43.

60% dynamite: *dynamite* is an explosive made from *nitroglycerin,* an oily liquid that is very explosive and highly sensitive to jolts, shocks and friction. To lessen the sensitivity and the dangers connected with it, nitroglycerin is mixed with an absorbent substance, such as sawdust or wood pulp, so that it is safe for handling, transporting, etc. This mixture is called *dynamite* and can be detonated by fire or sharp impact. Dynamite is produced in varying percentages, depending on the explosive power needed. A 60% dynamite would contain 60% nitroglycerin mixed with 40% absorbent substance. Page 95.

skin, under the: in essence; fundamentally; despite appearances or differences. Page 26.

slipstick: a device for making precise mathematical calculations, such as multiplication and division, consisting of a ruler with a sliding piece. Also called a *slide rule.* Page 10.

slither(s): a small, thin piece. Page 111.

slop chest: a store selling low-cost clothing, particularly for sailors. Page 25.

sluice(s): in mining, a long, sloping trough or the like, with grooves on the bottom, into which water is directed to separate gold from gravel or sand. Page 33.

sluicing pan: also *mining pan,* an open container for washing out gold, tin, etc., from gravel or the like, in mining. Page 36.

snap ending: an ending to a story that happens quickly and suddenly. Page 47.

soggy: sluggish; slow in responding. Page 61.

soldier of fortune: a person who independently seeks pleasure, wealth, etc., through adventurous exploits. Page 31.

souls, hearty: people of a particular type, in this case physically vigorous, strong and well. Page 53.

soup: 1. a slang word for *nitroglycerin,* a highly explosive liquid used in making dynamite and other explosives. Page 49.
2. additional power, from the slang term for a substance injected into a racehorse to speed it up. Page 85.

soupçon: a very small amount of something. Page 112.

sourdough: a prospector or settler, such as from the western US or Canada, so called because sourdough bread was often a major part of the diet. Sourdough bread is so called because it is made with a small portion of dough left over from the preceding day's bread baking. This small piece of dough causes the new day's bread to rise, giving the bread its familiar rounded shape. By keeping some dough from one day to the next, the dough develops a distinctive sour taste that it gives to each day's bread. Page 29.

South Seas: 1. the name given by early explorers to the whole of the Pacific Ocean. More usually applied to the islands of the central and South Pacific. Page 42.
2. (south seas) a reference to the Atlantic and Caribbean waters where LRH's Caribbean Motion Picture Expedition sailed. Page 84.

spewed: flowed in large amounts; gushed. Page 107.

Spirit of St. Louis: the name of the airplane piloted by American aviator Charles Lindbergh (1902–1974) on the first solo nonstop flight across the Atlantic on 20 May 1927. Lindbergh's 3,610-mile (5,810-kilometer) flight from New York to Paris, which took 33 hours and 32 minutes in this small single-engine airplane, was financed by businessmen from the city of St. Louis, Missouri, a city in the central United States. Page 84.

spitting: thrusting a spit (or something like a spit) through something. Literally, a *spit* is a pointed metal rod for holding meat and other foods while cooking before or over a fire. Hence *"spitting heathens,"* an ironic reference to earlier practices of burning alive individuals who held beliefs contrary to those of the early Christian Church. Page 42.

Sportsman Pilot, The: a monthly American aviation magazine published from around 1930 until 1943. It contained writings on a wide range of subjects, including coverage of aerial sporting events, commentary on current aviation issues, technical articles on flying and other articles on topics of general interest. Page 54.

squalls of anises: sprigs (small stems bearing leaves) of the *anise,* a fragrant Mediterranean herb of the parsley family, used as a seasoning and garnish. Page 111.

square: direct and straight. Page 45.

squeak, narrow: an escape from danger, destruction or the like by a very small margin or with difficulty. Page 23.

stalling: (of an aircraft) diving suddenly because of losing *lift,* the upward force of air on the wings that keeps the aircraft up as it moves forward. Lift can be lost when the aircraft moves upward (climbs) at too steep an angle or when its forward motion slows down too much. Page 57.

Stanford Research Institute: an independent, nonprofit research organization located in Menlo Park, California. Founded in 1946, the institute was originally associated with Stanford University (an institution of higher learning, founded in 1885 and located in Stanford, California). Page 128.

starboard: the right-hand side of a boat or ship as one faces forward. Page 107.

St. Croix: the largest of the Virgin Islands of the United States. *See also* **St. Thomas.** Page 17.

Stefansson: Vilhjalmur Stefansson (1879–1962), US explorer who discovered new regions of the Arctic and investigated the native cultures. He explored Iceland in 1905 and then led an expedition (1913–1918) into Canadian and Alaskan Arctic regions. In his numerous published works, Stefansson presented the Arctic as not only a hospitable place, but also an area of great military and strategic importance. Page 99.

Stetson: a type of felt hat with a broad brim and a high crown, particularly popular in the Western US. Named after John B. Stetson (1830–1906), who originated it in the mid-1800s. Page 10.

stint: a period of time spent doing something. Page 8.

stoop to: do something that is not in keeping with what one sees as one's own importance or worth; lower oneself. Page 33.

stope: a steplike excavation made in a mine consisting of both vertical and horizontal shafts to provide access to a steeply inclined or vertical vein (a layer of deposited mineral in the rock). Page 49.

strake: each of the continuous lines of planking in the side of a vessel, extending from the front (bow) to the back (stern). The *top gunwale strakes* are the top lines of planking that form the *gunwale* (or *gunwales*), the top edge of a ship's sides that forms a ledge around the whole ship above the deck. Page 107.

strangled (one) with fire: made the throat feel as though painfully burnt, to the point where it seemed to block the breath, by having a strong substance, such as whiskey or the like, poured down (one's) throat. Page 64.

struts: bars forming part of a framework and designed to give strength and support. Page 54.

St. Thomas: one of the Virgin Islands of the United States, a group of islands in the northeastern Caribbean Sea consisting of three large and several smaller islands. A colony of Denmark during the eighteenth and nineteenth centuries, the islands were purchased by the US in 1917. Page 17.

stubble field: a field covered with *stubble,* stumps of cut grain or hay remaining after harvesting. Page 82.

succor: help, relief, aid, assistance. Page 35.

Sudan: a region in north central Africa, south of the Sahara. An area of grasslands that extends across the continent, the Sudan is approximately 1,000 miles (1,600 kilometers) at its widest point. Page 111.

Sunday joy riders: people taking a pleasure drive on a Sunday. Page 61.

swamping: filling with water and sinking. Page 107.

swilled: washed by flushing with water. Page 112.

Tanit: ancient goddess of fertility. Page 118.

tarheel: a syrup made of molasses and maple syrup. Page 10.

tattle (upon): report on another's wrongdoing; reveal other people's secrets. Page 42.

tea-hound: a slang term for those of high society known to socialize rather than work. Page 17.

temperamental: unpredictable in behavior, likened to a person who is liable to unreasonable changes of mood. Page 24.

terra firma: solid ground. From Latin, literally meaning firm land. Page 77.

Terra Incognita: an unknown or unexplored land, region or subject. The term is Latin for "unknown land." Page 117.

Test Pilot: an LRH story first published in *Argosy* magazine in October 1936. An irresponsible pilot, confronted with the ultimate trial of courage, sacrifices his own life to save his younger brother. Page 91.

that there: a phrase used in some dialects as a way of saying *that* with emphasis. Page 61.

them's: an informal use of *them,* here meaning *them is,* a variation of *they are.* Page 73.

thyme: a plant with white, pink or red flowers and small leaves that have a sweet smell. The leaves are used fresh or dried as a flavoring in cooking. Page 111.

Timbuktu: a city in central Mali, a country in northwestern Africa on the southern edge of the Sahara Desert. Founded in the late eleventh century A.D., Timbuktu became a center of Islamic learning. The name of this city is often used in phrases to represent a place that is very far away. Page 10.

Toledo blade: a sword blade made in Toledo, Spain, a place famous for manufacturing sword blades of remarkable strength and toughness. Page 42.

tongue away from the cheek, keep the: mean something seriously, the opposite of the phrase *tongue in cheek,* intended as a joke, as if one were putting one's tongue in one's cheek while saying something, a gesture indicating that the remark is not meant seriously. Here used with a pun on *tongue,* in reference to the cows licking the wings of the plane. Page 79.

topsail: a sail set immediately above the lowermost sail of a mast. Page 21.

top sergeant: a noncommissioned officer who holds a senior position administering a unit of the US Marine Corps. *Noncommissioned* means not having a commission (a document awarding rank and authority issued by the president of the United States). Page 84.

torpedoes, damn the: a reference to an exclamation made by American naval officer David Farragut (1801–1870), who won fame in a battle of the American Civil War (1861–1865). After witnessing another American ship sink after striking an explosive device floating near the surface of the water, called a torpedo at the time, Farragut shouted, "Damn the torpedoes! Full speed ahead!" and led his ships through to victory. Page 95.

tow, in: in the state of being *towed,* pulled along by another vehicle. Page 62.

trailing: going off into something else, here used to describe the period of decline of the Roman Empire. *See also* **Roman Empire.** Page 124.

transit: an instrument with a telescope on top, employed in measuring land and in calculating angles and lengths. Page 10.

trawler: a commercial fishing vessel employed in fishing with a *trawl net,* a large, baglike net that is dragged along the sea bottom behind the ship. Page 120.

Treaty of Versailles: the treaty that officially ended World War I (1914–1918), signed in the city of Versailles in north central France. Besides requiring Germany to give up land and pay large amounts of money for damages, the treaty also reduced the size of Germany's army and navy and banned the manufacture of airplanes, tanks and submarines. Page 53.

tried: subjected to demands, requests or the like. Page 7.

Trinidad: an island country off the coast of South America, the most southerly of the West Indies. It consists of the two islands, Trinidad and Tobago, discovered by Christopher Columbus in 1498. Page 29.

troller: a *trolling boat,* one that is used to catch fish by means of trolling. *See also* **trolling.** Page 106.

trolling: fishing by trailing a baited line behind (a boat). Page 106.

Troy: an ancient city in Asia Minor (now Turkey) made famous in the legends of early Greece. Troy had long been regarded as a purely legendary city, but archaeologists in the late nineteenth century began excavations that unearthed the actual stone walls and defensive structures of an ancient city in the area where Troy was reputed to have existed and have since discovered numerous cities built on the same site. Page 118.

Tunis: a city and the capital of Tunisia on the north coast of Africa. Page 124.

Tunisia: a country in North Africa, on the Mediterranean. Page 122.

turns, by: one thing following after another. Page 70.

20th Marines: a reserve unit of the Marine Corps. Page 10.

twenty-two rifle: a rifle with a barrel that has the inside diameter of approximately one-quarter of an inch (.22 inch or 5.58 millimeters). Page 45.

twilight: the time when something is declining or approaching its end. From the literal meaning of *twilight,* the time of day just after sunset (and before full dark) or before dawn (and before full day), when the Sun is below the horizon. Page 21.

typhoon: a violent tropical storm of the western Pacific area and the China seas. Page 8.

Umpteen Airport: a made-up name. *Umpteen* means a large but unspecified number (of something). Page 69.

underbrush: shrubs, low vines, small trees, etc., growing under the large trees in a wood or forest; undergrowth. Page 35.

undergraduate: a student at a university or college who has not yet received a degree. Page 19.

undertaker: one whose business is to prepare the dead for burial and to arrange and manage funerals. Page 84.

under the skin: in essence; fundamentally; despite appearances or differences. Page 26.

underwrite: insure on life or property. Page 91.

unknown, fall before the: be ruined or defeated when facing something strange or unfamiliar, something that one knows nothing about. Page 1.

unvarnished: said or presented without any attempt to disguise the truth. Page 100.

upwards to: more than; in excess of. Page 35.

utility glider: another name for a *secondary glider*. A secondary glider or sailplane is built like an ordinary airplane and has a cockpit for seating one to two people. The wings are longer than those on a primary glider. Page 57.

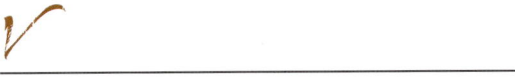

Valencia: a city in eastern Spain, founded in Roman times. Page 122.

vein: a layer of a mineral in rock, especially an ore or a metal. Page 35.

Versailles, Treaty of: the treaty that officially ended World War I (1914–1918), signed in the city of Versailles in north central France. Besides requiring Germany to give up land and pay large amounts of money for damages, the treaty also reduced the size of Germany's army and navy and banned the manufacture of airplanes, tanks and submarines. Page 53.

vest-pocket: small, from the idea of being small enough to carry in the pocket of a vest. Page 44.

V. F. D.: an abbreviation for Volunteer Fire Department. Page 77.

Vieques Sound: the channel between Puerto Rico and Vieques, a small island at the eastern end of Puerto Rico. Page 20.

voluble: characterized by a ready and continuous flow of words; fluent; talkative. Page 31.

voodoo: a body of beliefs and practices originally from Africa that includes magic and the supposed exercise of supernatural powers through the aid of evil spirits. Page 28.

Waldorf: a reference to the famous Waldorf-Astoria Hotel in New York City. Page 77.

wanderlust: an impulse, longing or urge to travel. Page 10.

Washington Monument: the tall, white-marble, four-sided stone pillar tapering toward its pyramidal top located in Washington, DC, which honors George Washington (1732–1799), the first president of the United States (1789–1797). It is 555 feet (169 meters) in height and is one of the tallest stonework structures in the world. Page 61.

Washington (State): a state in the northwestern United States, on the Pacific coast and bordering with Canada to the north. Page 4.

way: movement of a vessel through the water; velocity. Page 106.

wayfarer: a person who voyages from one place to another; traveler. Page 17.

West Indies: a large group of islands between North America and South America in the North Atlantic. Page 28.

White Horse: the brand name for a Scotch whiskey. Page 31.

whole track: the moment-to-moment record of a person's existence in this universe in picture and impression form. Page 118.

wildcat: of or relating to an activity, such as mining or oil drilling, that operates in areas not previously known to be productive. Page 31.

Wilkins: Sir George Hubert Wilkins (1888–1958), Australian explorer and aviator. He was part of an Arctic expedition (1913–1916) led by explorer Vilhjalmur Stefansson. In 1928 he made the historic first flight across the Arctic Ocean, from Alaska to Norway, an accomplishment for which he was knighted. Later that year Wilkins made the first Antarctic airplane flights while surveying the Antarctic Peninsula. Page 99.

willies: a strong feeling of nervous discomfort. Page 69.

windjammer: a large sailing ship. Page 84.

woe betide: an expression predicting great sorrow and grief for a person. *Woe* means misfortune, trouble or grief and *betide* means to happen to. Page 26.

woodlore: skill and practice in anything relating to the woods, such as camping, tracking, hunting and studying wildlife. *Lore* means accumulated facts, traditions or beliefs about a particular subject. Page 7.

working: performing its function and accomplishing expected results. Page 8.

workings: a place where a mineral is dug out of the ground. Where the mineral is located in or near a stream, the workings would include the dam and sluice used to wash the mineral out of the gravel that is dug up. Page 33.

wrassle: an informal variation of *wrestle,* struggle or fight with. Page 105.

yellow jacket: a wasp with black-and-yellow bands on its body. It nests in the ground or in the hollows of trees and can sting repeatedly. Page 110.

yoho: an exclamation used to call attention, originally as used on ships, and the line *"yoho and a bottle of rum,"* a phrase that calls to mind the pirates who once sailed throughout the Caribbean. The line is from *Treasure Island,* the 1883 novel by Scottish writer Robert Louis Stevenson (1850–1894), about a boy who finds a treasure map and sails off to Treasure Island, figuring to get the buried treasure before the pirates do. Page 26.

INDEX

A

Adventure
    Ron writing
        biographical notes, 2
        of civil engineering, 10

"Adventure is my guidon," 131

adventure(s)
    Caribbean expedition and, 23
    county fair and, 77
    Dianetics and, 117
    for sake of adventure, 91
    guidon, 131
    human spirit, ultimate realm of, 128
    in search of, 73
    in the heart, not in the view, 131
    learning to tell the lesser tale, 2
    1928 and second Asian, 8
    recipes for, 110
    tales from some forty years of, 1
    universe of You, 118

aerial photographer
    photograph of L. Ron Hubbard, 81

Africa
    East Coast of, 120

agriculture
    Puerto Rican brand of, 42

Alaska
    Kodiak bears known as brownies, 105

Alaskan Radio Experimental Expedition
    Explorers Club flag on, 100
    1940, 10, 84
    photograph of L. Ron Hubbard, 101

Albright, Richard W.
    portrait of L. Ron Hubbard, 48

Aleutians
    LRH braving 180-mile-an-hour winds, 100

Aleuts
    Ron's ethnological study of, 100

Alexander the Great
    "psychic" search for tomb of, 120

Alexandria Project
    Stephan A. Schwartz, 128

altimeter, 53

American
    kindliness and good fellowship, 77

America's National Archives
    LRH maritime notations in, 10

ancient world
　succumbing to internal strife and mismanagement, 126
Andersonville
　stop on flight with Flip, 79
Andrews, Roy Chapman
　descent into the Gobi, 100
Anglo-Saxon
　sites, 120
Antarctic
　Sir George Hubert Wilkins, first to fly, 99
Apollo 14
　Edgar Mitchell, astronaut, 118
Araby, 112
archaeologist
　fundamental error in counting soldiers, 126
Archbold, Richard
　Explorers Club and New Guinea exploration, 99
Arctic Circle fame
　Vilhjalmur Stefansson and, 99
Argonotes
　column in *Argosy*, 92, 93
Argosy, 54
　dangerous profession stories in, 49
　"Hell Job" series, 91
　　Ron's description of, 92
　Mr. Luck, 92
Arrow Sport
　adventure, Ron and Flip, 69
　biplane, 73
　map of route, 78
　1931 landing of, 84
artifacts
　finding and examining, 120

Asherat, 124
Asia
　1927, first of two Pacific voyages to, 8
　1928, second adventure to, 8
Atlantic
　Lindbergh crossing, 53
aviation
　Ron's 1936 *Test Pilot* on accurate aeronautical feats, 91
　sideshow to some, 73
aviator
　Ron Hubbard, 84
Avon River
　describing sites to crew, 124
　150-foot North Sea trawler, 120
　photograph, 120
　primary expeditionary vessel, 122
　survey parties studying clay models, 122

B

Baltimore
　Caribbean Motion Picture Expedition leaving from, 17
barnstorming
　craze, 69
　flying under every telephone wire in Middle West, 85
barracuda
　fishing in Sargasso Sea, 21
Barrio del Carmen, 44, 45
Beallsville, Maryland
　photograph of L. Ron Hubbard, 46
behavior
　physical pain and unconsciousness affecting, 117
Bermuda
　Caribbean expedition and, 25

Blackfoot medicine man
    acceptance of Ron as tribal blood brother, 2

blood brother
    Blackfoot medicine man and, 2

Boas, Franz, 100

Boubbouche, 111

Bou i laff, 112

British Columbia
    coast pilots with LRH notations of 1940 Alaskan expedition, 10

British Imperial Antarctic Expedition
    Sir George Hubert Wilkins and, 99

British Secret Service
    Major Ian Macbean from, 8

brownie, 100, 105, 107, 108
    see also **Kodiak bear**

Browning, Philip
    Caribbean Motion Picture Expedition, 17
    expedition and last-minute illness of, 19
    fellow aviator, 69

Buddhist lamaseries
    venturing into, 8

Bureau of Commerce
    Puerto Rico and head of, 31

Buried Alive!, 49

Butte School of Mines, 43

Buzzards
    George Washington University, 53

C

cable tool drilling, 94

camera
    Kodiak bear and no, 106

Canadian border
    Geological Survey, 10

Canary Islands
    Las Palmas, 122

Cantonese pirates
    encounter with, 9

Cape Orlando, Sicily
    ruins, 124

Capitol Hill
    United States Air Force, 84

car
    traveling in Nevada by car, photograph, 2

Caribbean Motion Picture Expedition, 17
    advertisement for, 17
    Doris Hamlin, full sail photograph, 14
    hard weather, photograph, 27
    map of route, 20
    Mount Pelée, photograph, 22, 23
    Murder at Pirate Castle and, 91
    1932, 10
    Philip Browning, 17, 19
    photograph of Captain L. Ron Hubbard, 16
    photographs, 21
    Salty Memo, 25

Caribbean recipe
    Iguana à Rotisserie, 110

Carib Indians, 38

Carper, J. B.
    mining engineer, 31

Carthage, 124
    map, 122
    ruins near, photograph, 129

Carthage patroness, 123

Cascades
    Ron leading a party of mountaineers, photograph, 4

Castellammare, Sicily
    ruins, photograph, 125

Catholicism, 28

challenge

"What is life without challenge?," 2

Chesapeake Bay

Caribbean expedition and sail-shredding winds, 20

Doris Hamlin, photograph, 14

Chicago airport

Ron flying around, 84

children

Tibetan and Indian, recall of former incarnations, 118

China

braving typhoons to finally land at, 8

digging for gold in Corozal by laborers from China, 38

Choua, 112

cinches

belonging with saddle, 45

civil engineering

Ron writing in *Adventure* on, 10

Classic Fiction Series

L. Ron Hubbard, 91

clay representations

missions and, 122

prospective sites and, 122

coast pilots

British Columbian, Alaskan expedition and, 10

Lesser Antilles, 20

West Indies, 99

cockpit

Franklin PS2 with closed, 53

primary having no, 61

College Park Airfield

LRH photographs, 50–51, 76

Columbia Pictures

Secret of Treasure Island and, 91

Columbus, 38, 42

West Indies and, 29

compass

wind as the only, 69

Congressional Airfield, 53

Franklin PS2 and, 84

Conquistadores

agriculture, 42

establishing customs in Puerto Rico, 42

gold in West Indies, 29

not telling natives that cinch belongs with saddle, 45

thirsting for gold and adventure, 40

cookbook

Explorers Club, 110

Coolidge, Calvin

thirteen-year-old L. Ron Hubbard and meeting the president, 4

coolie hat, 35

Corozal

Chamber of Commerce, 32

collecting samples near, photograph, 28

description, 36

Corozal River

members of a wildcat mining company, LRH photograph, 31

courage

men living not long without, 1

Crabtown, 10

crime

Spaniards and, 37

crises

expeditions failing for want of clear thinking, 117

criticism

technically descriptive stories and, 95

customs

adhering to, 42

D

Dare Devils
  Ohio farm boy and, 72
death
  L. Ron Hubbard inspecting mine, coming close to, 49
definitions
  "K jobs," 92
  whole track, 118
Department of Commerce Motorless Aircraft License 385, 57
Dianetics
  applicable to far-flung explorer and man on the street, 117
  application to expeditionary work, 117
  description, 120
  research toward development of, 10
  Terra Incognita and, 117
dope
  cows eating dope and fabric off the wings of planes, 79
Doris Hamlin
  Caribbean expedition and, 17–24
  full sail, photograph, 14
  hard weather, photograph, 27
  last of the four-masted schooners, photograph, 24
  photographs, 17–19, 21, 26
du Pont, Dick, 57
dying
  "Hot dawg!," 63
dynamite
  Puerto Rican native in charge of, 94

E

Eagle Scout
  America's youngest, 4
Egypt, 120
Elliott, Glenn
  flying instructor, 53
El Yunque
  jungle of, 43
***Enchanter*,** 123
  double-ended, high-sided ketch, 120
  photograph of L. Ron Hubbard aboard, 116
  photographs, 120, 121, 126
  scout, 122
engineer
  mining
    J. B. Carper of Washington, DC, 31
    living to tell the tale, 44
engineering
  studying, 10
epilogue
  "Adventure is my guidon," 131
***espiritismo*,** 28
ethnologist
  LRH known within exploratory circles as, 100
expeditions
  Caribbean, 1932, 10
  Caribbean Motion Picture Expedition, 17
  directing motion picture expedition, 31
  failing for want of clear thinking in crises, 117
  Mission into Time, 117
  Puerto Rican Mineralogical Expedition, 28
  Ron's first formal exploratory, 10
experience
  Ron's personal experience in order to shape a story, 91

exploration
    Scientology, Ron's primary track of, 128
    tales from some forty years of, 1

explorer
    strangest place an explorer can go, 117

Explorers Club
    banquets, 110
    bracelet of L. Ron Hubbard, 100
    examining Dianetics in name of, 117
    flag, 100
        honor to carry it, 100
        number 163, 120
        official sanction of exploratory ventures, 99
        reason for tattered state of Flag 105, 100
    founded 1904, 99
    home to greatest names in exploration, 98
    membership at, 99
    1940 Alaskan expedition and, 10
    photograph, 98
    Richard Archbold and New Guinea, 99
    stuffed polar bears and elephant tusks in, 99

Explorers Club anthology
    Kodiak bear story, 100

Explorers Cookbook: An International Potpourri of Recipes and Tales from World Adventurers, The, 110

Explorers Journal, The
    Terra Incognita appearing in, 117

F

Fairmile Class "B" Motor Launch, 120

fallacy
    writing technically accurately or bowing to, 95

fall before the unknown, 1, 131

fiction
    terminology evolved in, 93

First World War
    aerial knight of, 69

Five-Novels Monthly, 54

"Flash" Hubbard
    photograph of
        L. Ron Hubbard, 52
        L. Ron Hubbard and "Flip" Browning, 83
    world of aviation and, 84

fliers
    stout-souled, 77

flight
    four things proven in, 82
    thirty-minutes above Michigan, 69

Flip,
    see **Browning, Philip**

flying
    "precariously, and by the seat of your pants," 53

flying cap
    photograph, 57

flying wooden kimono, 61

fountain of youth
    Ponce de León and, 41

Franklin PS2 glider
    lessons in, 53
    photograph, 59, 62
    powerless ship, 84

friend
    warm faith in the might of, 1

G

Garfield, Captain
    "Aye aye! Sir!," 26

Caribbean expedition and, 20

garlic
Spanish food and, 36

"gaveta"
wooden pan, 35

Geological Survey
Canadian border, 10
Maine, 10

George Washington University
aeronautical gentlemen, photograph, 85
director of flying club, 85
formal education in, 10
Glider Club, 53

Giovinni
Ron decking Italian swordsman named, 9

Glenn, John
American astronaut, 110

gliders
American enthusiasm and, 53
flying, 84
Franklin PS2, 53
photograph, 59, 62
George Washington University Glider Club, 53
glider club, 60
license to fly, 54
photograph, 59, 60
pieces of glider all over terrain, 63
pilot log of flights, 63
Port Huron, Michigan, glider club, 54
primary, 61
secondary, 84
towed by Model A Ford, 61
towed by Model T Ford, 53
utility glider, 57

Gobi
Roy Chapman Andrews' descent into, 100

gold
alluvial
Corozal and, 32
existing in abundance, 33
diggings, Chinese and Spaniards, 38
learning of mining, 35
prospecting for
in wake of Conquistadores, 29
moral of story of, 47
separating black sand and, 36

gold miner, 84

Goldwater, Barry
US senator, 110

Great Depression
Caribbean expedition through, 17

Great Wall of China
LRH photographs, 10, 12–13

Greco-Roman ruins
photograph, 114–115

Greece, 120

groundlooping
sixty miles an hour, 77

Guam
engineering of a jungle road, 9
father serving at US refueling station, 8
photograph of L. Ron Hubbard, vi

Gulf of Aden, 120

H

Haidas
Ron's ethnological study of, 100

Hamilton, Don
flying instructor, 53

Index 181

Hammonds, 31
Hanks, Nancy, 2
    photograph of LRH astride, 2
Hartford Radio Relay League, 26
Hawks, Frank "Mr. Pilot"
    not above sailing powerless ship, 53
hazardous occupation stories, 93
health
    physical pain and unconsciousness affecting, 117
heart
    adventure is in the heart, 131
"Hell Job" series, 91–95
    Ron's description in *Argosy*, 93–95
hell raisers
    one of aviation's most distinguished, 85
Hillary, Edmund
    Mount Everest and, 100
hillman, 32, 37, 38, 45
history
    amplifying man's knowledge of, 120
honey-comb quartz, 38
horse
    Nancy Hanks, LRH's horse, 2
    Ron brought with him in Puerto Rico, 44
hospitality
    Middle West and, 77
"Hot dawg!"
    dying and, 63
Hubbard Geological Survey Expedition
    description, 120
    teams directed to buried ruins, 120
Hubbard, L. Ron
    portrait by Richard W. Albright, 48
human mind
    exploration into, 117
Hydrographic Office, 100

I

Ibanez, Don Martin
    Corozal Chamber of Commerce, 32
Iguana à Rotisserie
    Caribbean recipe, 110
    Central America, 113
Iliad
    Heinrich Schliemann and, 118
immortal being, 118
incarnations
    recall of former, 118
Incas
    Pizarro and, 41
Indian
    children recalling former incarnations, 118
industry
    Puerto Rico and ignorance of agriculture and, 38
"infinity of infinities, the," 128
Inside Passage
    photograph of L. Ron Hubbard en route through, 101
    recharting of, 100
insurance
    description of ratings on, 92
iron horse, 25
Italy, 120
"It Bears Telling"
    story, 105

J

jail
    Corozal, description, 37
Jamaica, 17
jibaros, 28
    boy on a horse, LRH photograph, 39

different races making up, 38

johnny cake, 10

Joplins, 31

K

Kentland, Indiana, 77

kimono, flying wooden, 61

kindliness

American, 77

"K jobs"

completely out and banned, 92

definition, 92

Kodiak bear, 100, 103, 106

Captain L. Ron Hubbard wrestling, 103

story of, 105

three-quarters of a ton of, 107

see also **brownie**

Kuril Islands

LRH photographing Japanese warships en route, 100

L

Lady Luck, Old, 60

Lafayette Escadrille, 69

lamaseries, Buddhist

venturing into forbidden, 8

landlubbers

Caribbean expedition and, 26

lands

exploring so many far-flung, 1

lure of strange horizons and faraway, 131

where men had to be big or fall before the unknown, 10

La Plata Mine Assays

LRH diagrams, 32, 33, 43

Las Palmas

Canary Islands, 122

LeBlond

Arrow Sport and, 69, 73

seemingly puny in expanse, 82

Lesser Antilles, 20

coast pilots, 20

Lewis II, H. Latane

aviation columnist, 84, 86–87

license to fly, 54, 57, 60

life

"What is life without challenge?," 2

lifetimes

"remembering" key archaeological sites from former, 118

Lindbergh

crossing Atlantic, 53

Spirit of St. Louis, 84

lives

Man possessing experience across many centuries and, 118

Livingstone, 117

Long Table, 103

LORAN

system, development of, 100

luck, 64

Lucky Lindy

not above sailing powerless ship, 53

Luquillo

village of, 43

M

Mac,

see **McBride, Thomas Finley**

Macbean, Ian

photograph, 9

young Ron and, 8

Italian swordsman, 9

Magician

schooner, 103

Maine
  Geological Survey, 10
malaria
  quinine for recurrent bouts of, 28
Man
  studying Man to understand him, 1
Manchuria
  tour of, 9
Mann, Bill
  Washington Zoo and, 103
maps
  Caribbean Motion Picture Expedition route, 20
  L. Ron Hubbard's major travels (1911–1929), 8–9
  Mission into Time route, 122
  Puerto Rico, 44
  route of the Arrow Sport, 78
  West Indies (Puerto Rican) Mineralogical Expedition route, 30
Marine Corps biplane
  photograph, 55
Marines
  Ron as top sergeant in, 84
  20th, brief service with award-winning, 10
Martinique
  Mount Pelée, 21, 23
    photographs, 22, 23
Maryland
  recuperating after Puerto Rico in, 45
Maryland air meet
  Marine Corps biplane, photograph, 55
McBride, Thomas Finley
  searching for ore with Ron, 43
McGraw, Mike
  nitroglycerin and, 94
  The Shooter and, 92

medicine man
  friendship with Blackfoot, 2
Mediterranean ports
  Mission into Time, 122
memory
  how retained and retrieved, 117
  whole track
    LRH-sketched maps from, 120
    tapping for archaeological advance, 120
    Temple of Tanit and, 124
"Men had to be big or fall before the unknown," 1, 131
metal detectors
  photograph, 128
Michigan
  about to explode over several acres of cow pasture, 61
  first flight landing in, 73
  thirty-minute motorized flight above, 69
Middle West
  barnstorming, flying under every telephone wire in, 85
  kindly curiosity of, 73
mind
  universe of, 128
mine assays
  LRH diagram, 32, 33, 43
mine shaft
  LRH rescued from, 49
mining
  gold
    in your own back yard, 47
    Puerto Rico and, 38
  world, 31
mining pans
  equipped with sample pick and, 31
  photograph, 36

Mission into Time, 117–129
    "A Test of Whole Track Recall," 122
    Cape Orlando, Sicily
        ruins, 124
    Castellammare, Sicily
        photograph of ruins, 125
    clay models, 122
    Greco-Roman ruins, photograph, 114
    inspiring several similar projects, 128
    LRH notes, 123
    map of route, 122
    mission policies and, 122
    photograph of L. Ron Hubbard aboard the *Enchanter*, 116
    ruins of Tanit, photograph, 123
    Tunis, 124
    Valencia, 122
Mitchell, Edgar
    American astronaut, 118
Model A Ford
    towing gliders, 61
Model T Ford
    journey through Rocky Mountains in, 4
    searching for adventure in, 73
    securing the Franklin's nose to, 53
Montana
    Butte School of Mines, 43
    living in, 2
    map, 9
    photograph of LRH astride Nancy Hanks, 2
Montana's 163rd National Guard
    second Asian adventure after, 8
Morton
    American engineer, 44
        mining, 1914, 44
Mother Hubbard
    natives of South Seas and, 42

Mount Everest
    Edmund Hillary's ascent of, 100
Mount Pelée
    ascending, 21
    photographs, 22, 23
    photographs purchased by *New York Times*, 23
movie director-explorer
    Ron Hubbard as, 84
Mr. Luck
    Argosy, 92
Murder at Pirate Castle
    Caribbean expedition and, 91
"Music with Your Navigation," 84

n

Nancy Hanks, 2
    photograph of LRH astride, 2
Nan-k'ou Pass
    Great Wall of China near LRH photograph, 10
National Archives, 10
National Guard, 8
National Museum
    Vieques Sound coral, 23
natives
    rescuing L. Ron Hubbard from collapsed mine shaft, 49
navy diver
    authenticity of story and, 95
Nebraska
    birthplace, 2
    map, 9
Nelson, Peter, 45
Nevada
    deserts and tires blowing out, 4

Ron Hubbard and father traveling
by car, photograph, 2–3
New London
stop on flight with Flip, 79
newspaper reporter
Ron Hubbard as, 84
New York Explorers Club,
see **Explorers Club**
New York Times
photographs of Mount Pelée
purchased by, 23
94th Aero Pursuit Squadron, 69
nitroglycerin
soup and, 92
Nora, Sardinia
Roman ruins
photograph, 119
North Pacific
driving logs down rivers of, 91

O

Ocean Archaeological Expedition, 120
Hubbard Geological Survey
Expedition, 120
O. Henry, 47
oil well stories, 94
Oklahoma
living in, 2
map, 9
Old Lady Luck, 60
O'Meara, Jack, 57
Orientalist
photograph of L. Ron Hubbard, 11
oxen
yoking of Puerto Rican, 42

P

Palo Blanco
honey-comb quartz and, 38
LRH photograph, 40
pan
wooden, "gaveta" and, 36
paranormal research
Edgar Mitchell, 118
past-life memories, 118
Peking
map, 8
photograph of L. Ron Hubbard, 11
tour of, 9
Pelée,
see **Mount Pelée**
Pennsylvania Railroad, 25
personnel
selecting expeditionary, 117
Phoenician-Carthage ruins, 124
piano wire
flying, crashing and, 64
pilot log, 63
first official solo flight, 79
pilot(s)
aeronautical gentlemen (1931),
photograph, 85
amazing rural townsfolk and, 69
flaming-haired pilot, Ron Hubbard, 84
gathered together around the nation's
capital, L. Ron Hubbard and, 84
glider pilot's license, 60
photograph of
"Flash" Hubbard, 52
L. Ron Hubbard, 65, 68, 72, 80–81,
85, 87
L. Ron Hubbard and "Flip"
Browning, 83

L. Ron Hubbard in a Franklin PS2
    glider, 59

recognized as outstanding, 85

United States informally toured by, 82

Pilot, The

photograph of L. Ron Hubbard, 87

"Who's Who," article on L. Ron
    Hubbard, 87

pirates

Ron's encounter with Cantonese, 9

Pizarro, 41

planes, light, 82

Podunk

Umpteen Airport in, 69

Ponce de León

first governor of Puerto Rico, 41

Port Huron, Michigan, 17, 60

glider club, 54

Pratt Street, 25

priests

West Indies and, 40

primary glider, 61

no cockpit, 61

open, 53

problem

million-dollar, 31

professions

list of "extrahazardous professions," 91

Puerto Rican Mineralogical Expedition

boy on a horse, LRH photograph, 39

collecting samples near Corozal,
    photograph, 28

first complete Puerto Rican
    mineralogical survey under US
    domain, 99

map of route, 30

photograph by L. Ron Hubbard, 42

under US jurisdiction, 28

see also **West Indies Mineralogical
    Expedition**

Puerto Rico

boy on a horse, LRH photograph, 39

Caribbean expedition and, 21

    alluvial gold and, 28

coming close to death in mine
    in, 49

difficult prospecting in, 38

dress of women of, 42

head of Bureau of Commerce, 31

map, 44

native in charge of dynamite, 94

photograph by L. Ron Hubbard, 34

studying history of gold mining in, 35

Puget Sound, 92

LORAN between Alaskan
    Panhandle and, 100

Q

quinine

recurrent bouts of malaria and, 28

R

radio

LORAN and navigation device, 100

radio crooner

Ron Hubbard as, 84

recipes for adventure, 110

Red Sea, 120

relics

finding and examining, 120

Rickenbacker, Eddie

94th Aero Pursuit Squadron, 69

Río Negro

closing our work on, 35

sluicing the, 33

Río Sabana
    panning gold from, 43
Rocky Mountains
    journey through in Model T Ford, 4
Rodriguez, Jose, 32, 35
Rojas, Pedro, 45
Roman
    ruins, 120, 124
        near Carthage, photograph, 129
        Nora, Sardinia, photograph, 119
Roman-Carthaginian ruins
    sketches of, 124
romance
    "And they say romance is dead!," 82
Ryan ST (Sport Trainer)
    brainchild of T. Claude Ryan, 84
Ryan, T. Claude
    design of Lindbergh's *Spirit of St. Louis*, 84

S

Saint-Pierre, Martinique
    Mount Pelée
        ascending, 21
        photographs, 22, 23
        photographs purchased by *New York Times*, 23
sample pick
    equipped with mining pans, 31
    tap of, 29
"Sample Pick Saga, A," 28, 29
    true yarn, 45
San Diego Airport
    LRH photograph, 71
San Diego, California
    map, 9
    traveling to, 4

San Germán
    map, 44
    Minillas mine of Trautman at, 45
    Puerto Rican mine in, 49
San Juan, Puerto Rico, 28, 31
    Corozal, southwest of, 32
    maps, 30, 44
Sardinia, 122
    Greco-Roman ruins, photograph, 114
    LRH notes from Mission into Time, 123
    Roman ruins, photograph, 119
    Ron sketching second century B.C. foundation, 123
Sargasso Sea
    barracuda fishing, 21
    map, 20
Sayer, 32, 33
    mining engineer, 44
Schliemann, Heinrich
    unearthing ruins of Troy, 118
schooner
    Asian journeys, 8
    Caribbean Motion Picture Expedition, 17
    Doris Hamlin, photographs, 14, 24
    Magician, 103
Schwartz, Stephan A.
    Alexandria Project, 128
    "psychic" search for tomb of Alexander the Great, 120
Scientologists
    recalling name from former lifetime, 118
Scientology
    first scientific explanation of spiritual matters, 117
    primary track of Ron's exploration, 128

quest for answers now found in, 1
research toward development of, 10

Scouting
America's youngest Eagle Scout, 4
L. Ron Hubbard indebted to, 7
photograph of L. Ron Hubbard, 5
Washington, DC, 4
White House and, 4

secondary glider, 84

Secret of Treasure Island, The
Ron's scripting of, 91

seven seas
plowed keel in, 118

shish kebab, 112

Shooter, The
1936 story, 92

Sicily, 122
Cape Orlando
ruins, 124
LRH sketches of domed Roman
tomb, 124
map, 122
ruins, photographs, 125, 126, 127

skills
thirteen-year-old L. Ron Hubbard
and, 4

sky surfboard, 61

sluice
description, 33

sluicing pans
photograph, 36

soaring
sport not taken lightly, 57

soup
nitroglycerin, 92

sourdoughs, 29

South China
gold diggings and laborers from, 38

South Seas, 42
expedition aboard an ancient
windjammer, 84

Spain, 29
colonizing West Indies, 40
map, 122

Spaniards, 29, 37, 38, 40, 41, 42
garlic, close to the heart of, 36

Sparrow
guarding the plane, 77
willing her up, 77

"Spinning In," 57

Spirit of St. Louis
Lindbergh's, 84

spiritual beings
immortal and infinite, 118

Sportsman Pilot, The
"Flash" Hubbard covered
in, 84
LRH articles appearing in, 84
"Tailwind Willies," 75
"Won't You Sit Down?," 69

spy
LRH nabbing enemy, 100

Stanford Research Institute
"psychic" experimentation, 128

St. Croix, 17

Stefansson, Vilhjalmur
Explorers Club and Arctic
Circle fame, 99

St. Thomas, 17

stunts
pilots and breath-catching, 69

submarines
Ron photographing coves and channels
able to harbor enemy, 100

survey
geological

Italy, Greece, Red Sea, Egypt, Gulf of Aden, East Coast of Africa, 120
party, confirming LRH sketches, 124
teams finding sites as precisely described, 126

T

"Tailwind Willies," 69, 70, 75

Tanit Tower
ruins, photographs, 119, 123

tarheel, 10

tea-hounds
need not apply, 26

Temple of Tanit, 123
Ron sketching, 123
ruins, photograph, 119

Terra Incognita
"half an inch back of our foreheads," 117
within us, 131

"Test of Whole Track Recall, A"
Mission into Time, 122

Test Pilot
Ron's experiences in aviation and, 91

385th American glider pilot license, 54, 60

Through Hell and High Water, 103
"It Bears Telling," 100, 103
1941 edition, 103

Tibet
children recalling former incarnations, 118

Timbuktu, 10

Toledo blades, 42

tourist material
need not apply, 26

Trautman, 45
engineer dying after fortune made in mining, 44

Treaty of Versailles, 53

Trinidad, 29

Troy
unearthing ruins of, 118

Tunis
Mission into Time, 124

Tunisia, 122
Roman-Carthaginian ruins, sketches of, 124
ruins near Carthage, photograph, 129

U

Umpteen Airport in Podunk, 69

United States
informally toured by pilots, 82
Puerto Rican mineralogical survey and, 28

United States Air Force
Capitol Hill and, 84
Ron's work to form independent, 84

United States Department of Commerce, 70

United States Navy
father serving in, 4
Hydrographic Office, 100
subsidy of "psychic" experimentation, 128

universe
moment-to-moment record of a person's existence in this, 118
of You, 118

unknown
"Men had to be big or fall before the unknown," 1, 131

utility glider, 57

V

Valencia
Mission into Time, 122

Vieques Sound
   coral, 21
      acquired by National Museum, 23
   map, 20
villain
   oil well stories and, 94
volcanos
   photographs from rim of active, 17
voodoo, 28

W

West Indies
   coast pilots, 99
   Conquistadores and, 29
   Corozal, standard village of, 36
   directing a motion picture expedition in, 31
   gold prospecting in, 47
   seeking illusive gold in, 29
   Spain colonizing, 40
West Indies Mineralogical Expedition, 28
   map of route, 30
   to Puerto Rico, 30
   see also **Puerto Rican Mineralogical Expedition**
White House
   L. Ron Hubbard representing American Scouting at, 4
whole track
   definition, 118
   LRH-sketched maps from memory of, 120
   memory of Temple of Tanit, 124
"Who's Who"
   L. Ron Hubbard, 87
wild animal cages
   "K jobs" and Ron entering, 91
Wilkins, Sir George Hubert
   Explorers Club and, 99
windjammer
   expedition aboard, 84
"Won't You Sit Down?"
   The Sportsman Pilot and, 69
world
   ancient, succumbing to internal strife and mismanagement, 126

Y

yarn
   true, "A Sample Pick Saga," 45
You
   universe of, 118

Z

zoo
   Washington, Bill Mann and, 103

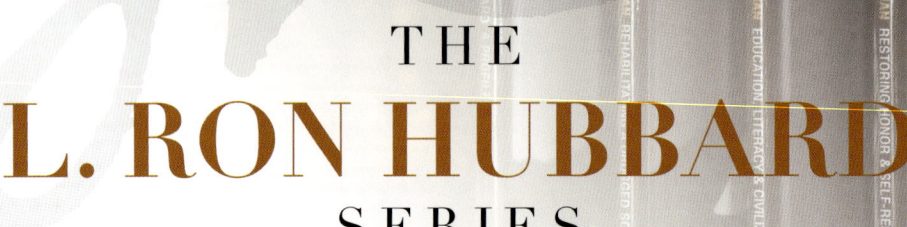

THE
L. RON HUBBARD
SERIES

"To really know life," L. Ron Hubbard wrote, "you've got to be part of life. You must get down and look, you must get into the nooks and crannies of existence. You have to rub elbows with all kinds and types of men before you can finally establish what he is."

Through his long and extraordinary journey to the founding of Dianetics and Scientology, Ron did just that. From his adventurous youth in a rough and tumble American West to his far-flung trek across a still mysterious Asia; from his two-decade search for the very essence of life to the triumph of Dianetics and Scientology—such are the stories recounted in the L. Ron Hubbard Biographical Publications.

Drawn from his own archival collection, this is Ron's life as he himself saw it. With each volume of the series focusing upon a separate field of endeavor, here are the compelling facts, figures, anecdotes and photographs from a life like no other.

Indeed, here is the life of a man who lived at least twenty lives in the space of one.

FOR FURTHER INFORMATION VISIT
www.lronhubbard.org

To order copies of *The L. Ron Hubbard Series*
or L. Ron Hubbard's Dianetics and
Scientology books and lectures, contact:

US AND INTERNATIONAL

BRIDGE PUBLICATIONS, INC.
5600 E. Olympic Blvd.
Commerce, California 90022 USA
www.bridgepub.com
Tel: (323) 888-6200
Toll-free: 1-800-722-1733

UNITED KINGDOM AND EUROPE

NEW ERA PUBLICATIONS
INTERNATIONAL ApS
Smedeland 20
2600 Glostrup, Denmark
www.newerapublications.com
Tel: (45) 33 73 66 66
Toll-free: 00-800-808-8-8008